BIBLE STORYING
FOR
CHURCH PLANTING

Daniel R. Sanchez

J.O. Terry

LaNette W. Thompson

Church Starting Network

Bible Storying for Church Planting

Copyright 2008 by Daniel R. Sanchez

Requests for information should be addressed to:

Church Starting Network
3515 Sycamore School Rd. # 125-161
Fort Worth, Texas 76133

www.churchstarting.net

smith_ebbie@yahoo.com

Library of Congress Cataloging-in-Publication Data

Daniel R. Sanchez, J.O. Terry, LaNette W. Thompson

Bible Storying for Church Planting

| ISBN: 0-9796254-8-3 | ISBN-13: 978-0-9796254-8-0 |

Cover design by: Daniel E. Sanchez
                  daniel@moonlight-studios.com

Printed in the United States of America

Other Books by the Authors

J.O. Terry:

Basic Bible Storying

Daniel R. Sanchez:

Starting Reproducing Congregations (co-author with Ebbie Smith)

Hispanic Realities Impacting America

Sharing the Good News with Roman Catholic Friends (co-author with Dr. Rudolph Gonzalez)

Gospel in the Rosary: Bible Study on the Mysteries of Christ

Church Planting Movements in North America (editor and Contributor)

Note: All of these books can be obtained from:

www.churchstarting.net

We dedicate this book to Dr. James B. Slack,
a pioneer in the design
of Chronological Bible Storying.
He has been a mentor and
a colleague to us and continues
to contribute to the development of this
instrument that the Lord is using to reach
untold numbers of oral communicators
around the world.

Preface by James Slack

Everybody loves a good story. This truth bodes well for those who like to tell stories and also means that there will always be ears waiting to hear the stories that storytellers tell. However, lest the persons hearing or reading these words think that the major historical and spiritual reasons for telling and hearing stories seeks primarily the entertainment of the teller and the hearer, another reality needs to be sounded. What many people do not know is that the current abilities and advances toward being literate for one-half to two-thirds of the world's people leaves them short of learning and communicating through any means than oral. Sadly enough, this awareness is especially lacking among those persons living in more literate settings and societies. The one-half to two-thirds of the people in the world who cannot read and write with understanding includes 45 to 55 percent of the people in Western nations. Oral individuals communicate and learn best, if not singularly, through hearing narrative presentations—stories and parables.

These facts being true, if one-half to two-thirds of the people in the world are to hear, understand, and have the chance to clearly respond to the gospel of Jesus Christ, gospel sharers should develop the ability to present the gospel to them in narrative-story formats. Jesus Christ understood this and, as individuals will learn from this book and from Mark 4:34, Jesus would not teach the common people without using a parable or a story.

It is exciting to me just how many Christian witnesses, teachers, preachers, and missionaries are now being introduced to the distinct realities of orality and literacy. This movement means that many are coming to understand these realities. It is even more exciting to see how many are now *"doers and not just hearers"* of the word as it is shared through Chronological Bible Storying. Consequently, Christian presentations concerning evangelizing the lost and discipling the believers through Chronological Bible Storying and other narrative approaches have been and are in the process of being developed for oral communicators and learners.

These communicators are actually employing these methods throughout the world. As encouraging as the narrative evangelism and discipleship presentations are, there is a concern that few oral and literate presentations are circulating in published form that provide mentoring, illustrations, and resources concerning planting churches through the Chronological Bible Storying approach. Their numbers are increasing and many are successful, such as is seen in the *One Story* and other similar projects.

This book is a much-needed presentation that will hopefully encapsulate the evangelism and discipleship functions within the church planting function. I trust this book will be widely circulated, but my primary prayer is that a majority of the readers will be enlightened to the point of being involved in planting multiple churches through Chronological Bible Storying. If this happens, this work will live more in its applied state than in its literate book state.

I know the authors of this book as productive practitioners and co-developers of the Chronological Bible Storying approach. I expect, therefore, its exposure to Christians will result in many literate church planters becoming sufficiently confident and skillful to go out and plant multiple churches through oral, narrative means. My prayer is that within the next few years the church planting approaches in this book will have been published orally through a number of generations of oral church planters. As this approach becomes a reality, the gospel will have traveled to the edges of lostness among the "*panta ta ethne*," the nations, the ethnic peoples of this world.

Dr. Jim Slack
May 2008

Preface by Grant Lovejoy

Bible Storying for Church Planting addresses a crucial topic. As more people learn about Bible storying, we need this focused instruction on how to use it to begin new churches. As the authors point out, we are more likely to succeed in starting new congregations through Bible storying when we have that outcome in mind from the beginning and act accordingly. Knowing that we want to plant multiplying churches in a particular community affects almost everything about our approach to Bible storying. *Bible Storying for Church Planting* reminds us about the factors we need to consider and tells how to incorporate them into our Bible storying and church starting.

Daniel Sanchez, J. O. Terry, and LaNette Thompson are an excellent team for writing such a book as this. Among them they have about a century's worth of experience as missionaries, trainers of church planters, and Bible storyers. They have decades of experience in the Americas, Asia, and Africa, respectively. They have planted churches in rural areas and in major cities like New York and Manila. They have drawn on those experiences and their network of contacts among successful practitioners in writing this book.

This book is not arm-chair theorizing; it reflects the ongoing dialog among people on the front lines of church planting. It includes honest admissions about situations in which Bible storyers failed to draw the net in evangelism, lacked intentionality in forming new groups, or drew on training and materials that were inadequate. But it also identifies the varied ways in which Bible storyers kept praying, experimenting, and adapting until they found a way to use Bible storying effectively in their situations. That experimentation continues around the world. *Bible Storying for Church Planting* offers a helpful snapshot of the current situation. It has launched a discussion that is likely to continue.

Grant Lovejoy
Director of Orality Strategies,
International Mission Board, SBC

Acknowledgements

We express our profound gratitude to some very special people whose contributions have made the writing of this book possible. Dr. Jim Slack, a true pioneer in Chronological Bible Storying (CBS)[1] has contributed to the development of CBS principles and methodologies and impacted everything that is done and will be done in this highly strategic missiological endeavor. We are also deeply indebted to Dr. Grant Lovejoy for his on-going contribution to CBS through his research, writings, and teaching. We sincerely appreciate the fact that he initiated the dialog regarding the question: "What can be done to ensure that Bible Storying contributes to the starting of more churches than ever before?" We express our gratitude also to LaNette Thompson who assisted us in gathering information from missionaries in Africa. In addition to sharing her valuable observations, she contributed a significant portion of chapter four in this book.

We acknowledge the valuable contribution made by the following missionaries who are serving in different parts of the world: These are: Christian J. Ammons, Donald Barger, Christi Brawner, David and Thora Broyles, Jackson Day, Tom Dyson, Steve Flook, Steven King, Fernando and Brenda Larzabal, Beth Severson, Keith Stamps, Ken Sorrell; Jeremy Taliaferro, and Mark Snowden (now with the North American Mission Board). These dedicated ministers graciously responded to our questions and provided excellent information and insights based on their firsthand experience with Bible Storying.

In a profound sense, the authors and the contributors discovered the insights in this book in their own experiences and in the testimonies of "storyers" on the fields. The principles were not dreamed up in offices. The ideas have come directly from persons engaged in the process of proclaiming the Message by storying. The many quotations from letters these hands-on contributors testify to their value to the study. The authors, therefore, express extreme gratitude to all those who have pioneered and practiced the use of this exciting method of gospel proclamation in all parts of the world.

We also want to express our profound gratitude to Ebbie and Donna Smith and to Keith and Penny Stamps for their valuable assistance in proofreading this manuscript for publication. Their gracious labor of love is deeply appreciated.

Contents

Introduction

We are seeing a good number of churches started in our area due to CBS strategies and we are seeing many churches that have been around for a while really begin to grow due to CBS strategies.

Jeremy Taliaferro, South America

The Miskito work is using CBS as a primary strategy and is seeing rapid church planting.

Keith Stamps, Central America

Students who have never started churches before are seeing multiple church starts now.

Christian Ammons, Asia

Bible Storying[2] is proving to be a marvelously effective tool for reaching oral communicators among people groups and population segments throughout the world. In light of the fact that two thirds of the world's population are oral communicators,[3] this methods of helping people hear, understand, internalize, and retell Bible stories is enabling missionaries and nationals to communicate the gospel message with untold numbers of persons who have not been reached through literate means.[4] Because of the efficiency of Bible Storying, communication bridges with highly resistant groups are being built and groups that have never heard the gospel message are receiving it. Evangelism, discipleship, and church starting are taking place among people groups and population segments in many areas of the world.

In certain countries missionaries and national workers find it necessary, or at least advisable, to use Bible Storying as an initial strategy among highly resistant people groups. LaNette Thompson, a missionary in West Africa, has discovered that Chronological Bible Storying (hence CBS) can be a very effective tool in reaching people who are hostile to the gospel. She explains: "If by giving a gospel presentation prematurely, you are going to create a barrier which will keep you from having an opportunity to share again, then storying is a way to break through these barriers." [5] This is consistent with an observation made by Wayne Dye who serves with Summer Institute of Linguistics International:

> People learn best in a non-threatening situation, because they can be more open to what is being taught. In a threatening situation, much of a hearer's unconscious energy goes into preparing to defend against the threat. A story presents concepts in a way that hearers do not feel obliged to agree with them. As a result, the new ideas are more likely to be accepted. [6]

An example of this is the way Bible storying opened the way for a missionary couple to share the gospel in a predominantly Muslim country. They had been praying and fasting for many days that the Lord would open a door. One weekend the husband was invited by a group of men to go out to the desert for the weekend. Their custom was to pitch tents at night, sit around a fire under the light of the stars, and tell stories. Sensing that this could be the opportunity they had been praying for, the missionary accepted the invitation.

As he sat listening to the stories that the men were telling he noticed several themes that kept surfacing in their stories: friendship, family, prayers, miracles, and heroes. After he had listened to many stories, the men asked him if he had a story to tell. Picking up on the friendship theme, the missionary told the story of David and Jonathan. [7] The men liked the story so much that they asked him if he could tell another story. He obliged by telling them the story of how King Hezekiah became deathly ill and he prayed to God and God extended his life by fifteen years. This sparked their interest even more and they asked him to tell another story. Focusing on the theme of family, he told the story of the prodigal son. At the end of the weekend those who had gathered went to their respective homes.

After a week, the leader of the group, who had invited him, came to the missionary's home and said: "Last night I had a dream that you were going to tell me a story about a holy person who is going to change my life." After the missionary told him the story of Jesus, this man became a believer and was instrumental in leading his family and friends to faith in Christ. This experience was the beginning of a house church in that country.[8]

J.O. Terry, who served as a missionary in South Asia, has noticed that many missionaries utilize Bible Storying to establish a beachhead among people who have never heard the gospel or among people who are resistant or even hostile to those who are seeking to share it. Their initial strategy is to establish listener groups who in time come to a saving knowledge of Jesus Christ and then gather into congregations. He explains: "We had many of these come out of several radio programs in India, both in the Khond Hills among the Kui, and farther south in Karnataka among the Kannada-speaking population."[9]

Mark Snowden has learned that Bible Storying is proving to be a highly effective instrument to reach isolated people groups. He shares an inspiring account of the way in which Bible Storying opened the door for Christians to enter a village where the gospel had never been shared before. He explains:

> My pastor, Ron Boswell, IMB missionary Gary Stone, and I were canvassing the Tajumulco (TAH-who-mool-co) Mam (mom) people to begin new work. We walked up the side of a dormant volcano to be the first Christians to enter an extremely remote, cloud-top village named Miraflores. It was brick-making day, so the village grandmother, mayor, and another leading citizen greeted us dripping in chunks of tan clay. They apologized profusely for their dirty clothes, but they were gracious to receive us. We were seated in an unused schoolroom and after a time of introductions, I had the opportunity to tell three Bible stories. Seizing upon their concern for their clothes, I first told

them the story of The Fall and played up the provision of animal skins to clothe Adam and Eve. I segued to Joseph's coat expressing the favor of a father and how that coat gave him a certain status among his eleven other brothers. I ended the storying session with a fast track story of the Trial, Crucifixion, and Resurrection to show the need to die for sins and bring the story to Jesus' promise to have the Holy Spirit come upon His disciples. By being clothed in His favor, we can have eternal life. My audience of three village leaders was very receptive and Gary did an excellent job tracking with me in storytelling interpretation. Each story took about 3 minutes to tell, so the whole "session" only lasted 15 minutes. However, it was well received. Our meeting resulted in opening the door for a first-ever outsider medical team and ongoing work that has resulted in at least one new church.[10]

This experience is not an isolated happening. In many parts of the world Bible Storying is providing an effective bridge to reach people who are initially ignorant of the gospel message or resistant to it.

In addition to this result, we rejoice over the fact that there are numerous places around the world where Bible Storying is being used as a very effective instrument to lead oral communicators to faith in Christ, to disciple them, and to gather into vibrant, reproducing congregations. Keith Stamps, International Mission Board Missionary (hence IMB) in Central America, states:

The Miskito work is using CBS as a primary strategy and is seeing rapid church planting. Closer to home, we have been training and encouraging a church plant in Villa Nueva, just outside Guatemala City. As we have worked with them on Storying they have made their own adaptations. Besides the growth of their own congregation, they are beginning works in rural El Salvador and encouraging multiple church plants in the Ixil triangle of Guatemala (Ixil language churches). When we introduced them to Bible Storying they took it up and have all been learning to tell stories from the Bible. This multiplies their potential and makes for more natural opportunities to witness and counsel in both urban and rural environments.[11]

Working as a missionary among indigenous groups in Mexico, Donald Barger has found in Bible Storying a most effective tool in reaching oral learners with the gospel and starting churches among them. He states:

We used storying to plant a church and to initiate work in several new locations that the nationals eventually developed into churches. Our worship services would be full of stories. In one of the churches the people would all tell a story during the services. Often they would just repeat the story that was told prior to their turn. It was great because it emphasized repeating the stories and total participation instead of just showing up and listening to one person. We have a couple of locations in Mexico now where we are seeing the first churches getting started using the stories. Our work there is young and most of our missionaries are early in their first term. It has been a great resource for getting into closed communities.[12]

Steven King, another IMB missionary is encouraged by the church planting efforts taking place in connection with Bible Storying strategies. He explains:

The Xtreme Team working in Peru and Bolivia among indigenous people groups has seen good first generation and some assisted second-generation church planting employing CBS. It is exclusively what they do.[13]

Jeremy Taliaferro, one of the Xtreme team leaders, is highly excited about the excellent response they have seen utilizing CBS in connection with their church planting efforts. He is especially positive about the incorporation of new believers into congregations through the methods of storying. He states:

> We are seeing a good number of churches started in our area due to CBS strategies and we are seeing many churches that have been around for a while really begin to grow due to CBS strategies. I feel this is mostly due to the power of Scripture, or the power of The Story. Storying is linked to real life. It shows the uncensored version of the Bible heroes. It shows us that God used people who were imperfect and he transformed them. It shows the rust in their armor. The Bible Characters remind the people of themselves and their families. It gives them hope of being used by God. And by showing the rust in their armor, the focus is redirected to a perfect God and his steadfast character. When you know the whole story it is hard to glorify the men of the story, but it is almost impossible to deny God the glory he is due. Another reason I believe we have seen so much success with CBS is because it gives them a job, a function from the very beginning, even before they are believers (to learn the story and tell it to others). When a church is finally planted the believers continue to function and share the story, because that is all they have ever known, it has become part of what it means to be a Christian to them.[14]

Missionaries, Fernando and Brenda Larzabal, serving in South America, have shared the exiting report of the mar-velous way in which the Lord is using Bible storying efforts in their part of the world. They explain:

> God has been doing incredible things in one of the people groups that we have been involved in. We want to share the story with you so that you can praise the Lord with us and pray

for the next steps for our national missionaries "L" and "J" (For security reasons we are using their initials). All of the People Group (hence PG) in the village where the national missionaries are working have heard the Bible story set at least twice. There was a unanimous group decision to become Christians (group decision making is part of their culture). "L" and "J" believe that there are about 25 very committed believers who have experienced powerful life changes. Twenty of them have been baptized. There are another 25 that they believe have also made a solid commitment.

There have been incredible changes in the lives of the PG. People were going hungry because they did not go out and collect food. They now go into the jungle and collect food for their families saying: "I'm going to get what God made for me." They are no longer afraid of the spirits that inhabit the jungle. They have learned to practice restitution for their wrong doings. Some have given chickens back to the people that they had stolen from. Drunkenness has disappeared from the village. They no longer want to drink. They want to hear the God stories.

One of the most powerful Bible stories for these people was the story of Jonah. They said: "We are like the people of Nineveh and we deserve to be punished by God." There is happiness and joy in a community where sadness and depression and suicide reigned.[15]

From Asia we are hearing very encouraging reports of churches being started through the use of Bible Storying. Christian Ammons enthusiastically shares:

Our time in Asia has been valuable. We used Storying exclusively to train leaders to train more leaders. One big difference this time is that we called for obedience and accountability from day one. The students had to teach everything they learned that day to someone on the street that same night. We had a much higher success rate than we had in the past, even though the students were in no way superior. Students that have never started churches before are seeing multiple church starts now.[16]

From India, Johnny Norwood has given the exciting news of the manner in which Bible Storying is being utilized as a powerful instrument for the salvation of many people and the establishment of churches in key villages. Norwood explains the experience of one of the participants:

I had never heard of the storying method before the seminar. Now I go to villages and tell the Old Testament and New Testament stories and God is working, bringing many Hindus to the Lord. Other churches in other villages have asked me to come train them in this method. I went to visit some Christians in a village. After praying and seeing God heal some of them, I began telling the stories. Some Hindus listened and requested that I come to their homes to tell stories also. Using storying I have started four other groups in villages with more than twenty in each group.[17]

Rick Brown shares the exciting news of a house church planting movement that is taking place in a predominantly Muslim country. He states:

Bible Storying in the form of a Creation to Christ (C2C) presentation has contributed to a people movement among Sufi Muslims. The sovereign working of God to prepare the leader of the Sufi movement and the supernatural work of the Holy Spirit are very evident. God had also pre-pared a Muslim Background Believer (MBB) who led the Sufi holy man into the true path of sal-vation using a story that spanned from creation through the exaltation of Jesus.[18]

Emphasizing the importance of taking the worldview of a people group into account in selecting the Bible stories that are to be shared and the strategy that is to be used, Dr. Lovejoy gives an example of how this is being done in that Muslim culture. He explains:

> The article's summary of this Creation to Christ (C2C) presentation indicates that the MBB included many familiar stories. But the MBB highlighted certain *worldview-specific themes*, too: The eight sons of Abraham; the disobedience of David's sons until a true son of David was born; Jesus as the true heir of the promises to Abram; Jesus as the first human being to be completely submissive to God; Jesus' death being the will of God. These worldview-specific themes presumably made the message more meaningful to the Sufi master.[19]

By way of summary, Lovejoy adds: "This is a strong encouragement to have a worldview-specific C2C presentation ready for the moment when God opens hearts to listen."[20]

As we have seen in the examples described above, it is evident that Bible Storying is being used as a very effective tool for church planting in many parts of the world. *In keeping with our desire to encourage and assist these efforts, our book focuses primarily on three target groups: 1) People who have not been involved in Bible Storying and want to utilize it as a church planting strategy from the beginning of the process; 2) People who are using Bible Storying as an initial strategy and want to proceed seamlessly from a storying group to a vibrant church;* [21] *and 3) People who want to explore the possibility of utilizing Bible Storying in combination with other church planting methodologies.* In an effort to accomplish these goals, we will focus on: Equipping the Storyer for Effective Church Planting; Understanding the Setting for Effective Church Planting; Developing the Strategies for Effective Church Planting; and Selecting the Stories for Effective Church Planting.

Chapter 1:
Equipping the Storyer

*Since God as revealed in the Bible has assigned the highest priority to bring men into living relationship to Jesus Christ, we may define mission narrowly as **an enterprise devoted to proclaiming the Good News of Jesus Christ and to persuade men to become His disciples and dependable members of His Church**.*

Donald McGavran

People need to understand that Bible storying is a discipline that requires effort, exercise and patience.

Keith Stamps

What is sad is that there may be some settings in which people are ready to begin to function as a body of believers but the Bible storyers either do not have the sensitivity to detect this or the skills to enable it.

Daniel R. Sanchez

The Bible Storyer is the most vital component in starting churches among oral communicators. Communication never occurs in a vacuum. The knowledge, personality, vision, and passion of the Bible Storyer are absolutely essential for churches to be started among a people group or population segment. In addition to obtaining the valuable information and acquiring the skills that are essential to be effective, the Bible Storyer needs to have a focused commitment to win, equip, and enable people to start vibrant, worshipping congregations in their cultural contexts. Among the factors that will contribute to this imperative undertaking are: A Solid Biblical Foundation; A Clear Harvest Theology; A Compelling Vision for Church Planting; A Working Knowledge of Church Planting Models; A Purposeful Plan; and An Unwavering Commitment.

A Biblical Foundation

A solid biblical foundation is the first factor necessary for church planters who desire to use storying as a method. Bible storyers will be effective only to the degree to which they have a solid biblical foundation for church planting and a clear understanding of the basic principles of Bible Storying. Several concepts contribute toward the attainment of this solid biblical foundation: 1)The recognition of the extensive utilization of oral approaches in Scripture; An understanding of the connection between the Great Commission and church planting; and A Knowledge of church planting patterns in the book of Acts.[22]

Recognition of Orality
in Scripture

A solid biblical foundation for church planting and storying begins with the recognition of orality principles in Scripture. This recognition of the utilization of oral approaches in Scripture can be both highly instructive as well as deeply inspiring for those who are seeking to reach oral communicators. In their book, *How To Read The Bible For All Its Worth*, Gordon Fee and Douglas Stuart point out that the Bible contains more of the literature called "narrative" than it does any other literary type. They explain:

> For example, over 40 percent of the Old Testament is narrative. Since the Old Testament itself constitutes three-quarters of the Bible, it is not surprising that the single most common type of literature in the entire Bible is narrative... It is our presupposition that the Holy Spirit knew what He was doing when He inspired so much of the Bible in the form of narrative. We think it is obvious that this type of literature serves God's revelatory purpose well.[23]

Limitations of time and space will not allow us to explore the use of stories in many of the books of the Bible. We will, however, give a brief overview of the use of stories in the Gospel of Mark. Many biblical scholars affirm that the Gospel of Mark is essentially a collection of the stories (*chreiai*) and sayings (*logia*) of Jesus that Peter could "recall from memory and relate from memory."[24] These writers view Mark as the "interpreter" in the sense that he received the stories and sayings from Peter and put them in written form that conformed to an oral style in his Gospel. It was not unusual for Mark, as he wrote the Gospel, to employ the short narratives he received as Peter related them from memory. He utilized brief anecdotes for educational purposes as he penned this Gospel. Richard Bauckham explains:

> In a predominantly oral culture everyone was familiar with various forms of relating short narratives or reporting sayings and would adopt such forms without needing to reflect on the matter at all... Education would simply heighten self-conscious reflection on the forms of anecdotes in persuasion and argumentation.[25]

This form of storytelling is evident in the Gospel of Mark. Bauckham further teaches:

> Certainly, within the Gospel of Mark, the content of the traditions is narrative and not a speech... The Gospel doubtless aims to persuade, but only in a way a narrative can do, quite differently from the way a speech can... There is no reason why Peter could not have given many of the *chreiai* in Mark their basic forms in his oral rehearsing of the words and deeds of Jesus.[26]

While some scholars[27] fail to see any kind of formal aesthetic arrangement in Mark's Gospel, Bauckham, along with others, supports the idea of a chronological arrangement of the narratives in this Gospel. He suggests:

> It is certainly true that the Gospel is largely composed of discrete narrative units and that often they are linked by no more or little more than "and" (*kai*). However, it is also obvious that they are not placed randomly together. There are, for example, topical collections

(controversial stories in 2:1-3:6 and 11:27-12:40; parables in ch. 4). There is the overall chronological framework of the transition from the ministry of John the Baptist to that of Jesus (1:4-15) and the death and burial of Jesus and the empty tomb... In the passion there are many episodes that, for causal or chronological reasons necessarily belong in the sequence that Mark presents.[28]

In the Gospel of Mark we not only see the use of stories to communicate biblical truth but the arrangement of these stories in chronological (or causal) order to enable the listeners to understand the basic truths and the significance that is revealed in the events in the life of Jesus. A study of Mark's Gospel also reveals that Mark took into account the intended audience in the presentation of the stories. Joanna Dewey makes this assertion:

> [T]he Gospel of Mark works well as oral literature. It is of an appropriate length for oral performance. A storyteller could learn it from simply hearing it performed. As I and others have argued elsewhere, its composition consists of oral composition techniques. Briefly, the story consists of happenings that can be easily visualized and thus readily remembered. It consists of short episodes connected paratactically [i.e., by no more or little more than "and," thus placing events side by side rather than subordinating one to another]. The narrative is additive and aggregative [short narratives accumulate rather than creating a climactic linear plot]. *Teaching is not gathered into discourses according to topic but rather embedded in short narratives, which is the way oral cultures remember teaching.*[29] [Emphasis ours]

Dewey makes a strong case for the argument that the manner in which Mark arranged the content of the stories was consistent not only with the order in which they occurred in the life of Jesus but with the learning capacity of what was largely an oral culture. This consisted of not structuring the material toward a "linear climactic plot" (to kill Jesus) but arriving there through "repetitive patterns." She further explains:

> Such structures are characteristic of oral liter-atures, helping the performers and audiences to remember and transmit the material. From what we know of oral literature there is no reason why it could not have been composed and transmitted in oral form. [30]

Evidence indicates that Mark's Gospel was written in a way that took the oral communicators into account and could be used for an oral performance. Bible Storyers can, there-fore, learn and apply many principles and methods to their particular storying strategies. The observations of Bauckham and Dewey regarding the Gospel of Mark provide a founda-tion for communicating with oral learners. These principles include:

- The employment of brief narratives for oral perform-ance;

- The short episodes that are placed side by side to help the listeners accumulate the information;

- The teaching that is embedded in the short narratives instead of being presented as topics;

- The sequence in which these are arranged to communicate the truth the listeners need to internal-ize;

- The employment of oral technique that helps the listener to visualize and remember the stories;

- The repetitive patterns employed instead of a linear approach.[31]

These principles allow oral learners to remember and transmit what they have heard. This truth helps us affirm that the first Gospel was written in such as way as to take oral communicators and communication among such peoples into account. We, therefore, have ample justification and motivation to emulate this example in our day.

The Great Commission and
Church Planting

Every church planting effort is such an awesome and demanding task that it must be solidly based on a strong biblical foundation. The biblical foundation for church planting of necessity must include commitment to the Great Commission of Christ (most fully stated in Matt. 28:18-20). Planting reproducing churches clearly finds expression in this commission. As we examine the Great Commission we need to focus on the authority, the imperative, the scope, and the promise.

The Authority

Often people start the Great Commission with the words "Go and make disciples." It is extremely important that we start at the beginning, where Christ speaks about *his* authority. "All authority has been given unto me in heaven and on earth." (v. 18) This statement means that no area, no people, or culture lies outside the domain of his power and authority. Having arisen, he now has exalted authority over the whole world.

It is important to note that authority precedes mandate. We must keep in mind that the mandate does not come from someone who wishfully hopes that somehow we might be able to fulfill it. It comes from the resurrected, exalted, empowered Christ who is capable of providing all of the resources that his people need to fulfill his command.

The Imperative

After making it clear that he has all authority, Jesus gave the missionary mandate: *"As you are going, make disciples, of all nations, baptizing them in the name of the Father and of the Son and of the Holy Ghost, and lo I am with you always, even to the end of the world"* (v. 20). In the Greek, the words "going, baptizing, and teaching" are all participles, helping verbs. The imperative, the command, (*"matheteusate"*) is **make disciples**.

The command of Christ involves more than getting people to register decisions. This attainment is but the starting point. Making disciples involves leading people to receive

Jesus as Savior and Lord, to become an integral part of His church as life-long followers, learners, and ministers, and working toward the spread of his kingdom. The commission Jesus gives his church involves evangelizing and discipling that is winning and developing.

The Scope

Jesus clarified the scope of the mission, saying: "*Make disciples of all nations.*" The word in the Greek for "*all nations*" is "*ta ethne*" from which we get out word "ethnic." This teaching means that all people groups need to be reached with the gospel and discipled. In order to implement the command, the followers of Christ must cross linguistic, sociological, racial, cultural, religious, ideological, generational, and geographical boundaries. Another way of stating this truth is that churches need to be planted among all of the population segments of the societies of the world. Every barrier to the gospel needs to be bridged by establishing churches that are near the unchurched, not only geographically but socially and culturally.

The Promise

As we look at chapters 16 and 18 of Matthew, we find two powerful and reassuring promises. First, Jesus promises to build his church. In Matthew 16:18 Jesus stated: "*I will build my church and the gates of hell will not prevail against it.*" It is clear from this passage that the establishment and expansion of the Church is first and foremost a divine endeavor. Jesus has promised to build *his* church and he never made a promise that he could not keep. It is also important to note that the picture that Jesus gives of his church is not one that defensively survives the onslaught of the enemy but one that aggressively tears down the strongholds of the enemy and rescues people with the gospel of salvation. Jesus promises to build his church and to protect, preserve, and perpetuate it.

Second, Jesus promises to be with his followers as they obey his command: "*Lo I am with you even to the end of the age.*" Jesus has promised to be with his disciples and with his church until he brings human history to the end he has determined. These promises hold true for all time. There will not be a time when he will not be with his followers who are doing his will and obeying his command. Followers of Jesus will never arrive at a place or experience a time when they are alone. He will not only be present but he will be there to guide and protect his followers in the task that he has commanded them.

The expression, "*to the end of the age*" assures us that he will not rescind his command until he has accomplished his purpose. It also assures us that there will not be a time when his power is curtailed. His church has gone through many trying times throughout her long and arduous history but his true followers have never been without his presence.

The term *all* holds tremendous significance in the Great Commission. Let's look for a moment at the ways in which the word "*all*" is used in the Great Commission. Jesus speaks of *All* power, *all* peoples, *all* the commands, and *all* of the time. In other words, the one who has *all* the power sends us to make disciples of *all* people groups, teaching them *all* of the things he has commanded us, and he will be with us *all* of the time.

How did the disciples make disciples? They did so by establishing churches. The disciples, without a doubt, thought of the way in which Jesus had discipled them. He had shared with them the message of the kingdom, invited them to follow him, spent time instructing them, praying with them, having fellowship with them, and then them sent out to make disciples. When the disciples, therefore, dedicated themselves to the task of implementing the command of Jesus, they thought not only about communicating the message but also about gathering the people so that they would form a fellowship in which the believers could continue to grow spiritually.

Church Planting in Acts

The Book of Acts contains many exciting and instructive stories about the planting of churches in different parts of the first-century world. From the story of the founding of the Jerusalem Fellowship we can learn what the basic functions of a church are. The Antioch church provides an example of a congregation that took the Great Commission seriously. An analysis of the methodology employed by Paul can be very instructive regarding the manner in which a church planter can be involved in starting indigenous, reproducing congregations.

The Church in Jerusalem

This church was born in a prayer meeting in the upper room of a private house in the ancient and historic city of Jerusalem. Christ had commanded his disciples to return to the city and await the coming of the Holy Spirit. Out of that group of humble disciples waiting in faith and obedience, God brought the church into being. From its inception, the Church, endued with the Holy Spirit, was given the spiritual gifts it needed to carry out its functions as a local expression of the body of Christ. We see in this infant church, therefore, the functions it needed no only to survive but to thrive. In Acts 2:40-47 we see a description of these functions:

- There was *proclamation*, both through testimony and preaching (v. 40).

- There was *incorporation*. Those that believed were baptized and added to the church (v. 41).

- There was *discipleship*. "They persevered in the Apostle's doctrines" (v. 42).

- There was *fellowship*, both the agape meal and the Lord's Supper (v. 42).

- There was *prayer*. They persevered in prayer (v. 43)

- There was *worship*. They worshipped God (v. 47). The presence of the Lord was among them in a tangible way (v. 43).

- There was *ministry* for they voluntarily sold of their possessions and shared their resources with those who were in need (v. 45).

- There was cultural identification in that "they found favor with the people" (v. 47).

- There was *propagation* of truth that is seen in fact that the Lord was *adding daily those who were being saved* (v. 47).

As we look at the functions of this church, it is important to point out that even though the methods may change, the functions remain vital to the life and ministry of the church. There was sensitivity to the Holy Spirit; at every juncture the church sought the guidance of the Holy Spirit. "The church in Jerusalem continued to be a church at prayer, obeying Christ's commands and seeking the power of the Holy Spirit at every step."[32] There was also a strong commitment to lay a solid doctrinal foundation. Aware of the fact that the Lord had commanded them to *"make disciples"* and to *"teach them whatsoever I have commanded unto you"* (Matt. 28:19, 20), the Apostles took great care to establish the Jerusalem Church upon the teachings of Christ. We see evidence of this when the new church *"persevered in the apostles' doctrines"* (Acts 2:42). These were not their own teachings but those they had received from Christ. There was great care to carry out the functions of the church (Acts 2:40-47) based upon the foundation that had been established.

The Church in Jerusalem, therefore, was a church which came into being by the will and power of the Holy Spirit as people heard the proclamation of the Gospel of the risen Savior and responded to it by deciding to become active members of the local expression of the body of Christ which had the task of implementing the Great Commission. The Apostles were the instruments of the Holy Spirit in the establishment of this church. We need to remember, however, that the establishment of the church was the birthright of those who had heard and responded to the Gospel.

The Antioch Church

After the establishment of the church in Jerusalem, other churches were established in Judea and Samaria in keeping with the promise of Jesus (Acts 1:8). In Acts 11:19 we read *"those who were scattered because of the persecution that rose in connection with Stephen made their way to Phoenicia and Cyprus and Antioch."* These believers were Jewish Christians who had been forced to flee the persecution but who were not hesitant to preach the Gospel at Antioch. Their preaching was confined *"only to the Jews."* In Acts 11:20, we read of another group. These were *"men of Cyprus and*

Cyrene who came to Antioch and began speaking to the Greeks also, preaching the Lord Jesus." These were quite likely Jews from the *diaspora* who were in Jerusalem on the day of Pentecost who returned to the lands where they lived perhaps due to the persecution in Jerusalem but later made their way to Antioch. Their sharing the gospel to the Gentiles expanded the vision and ministry of this church to be more in line with the mandate of the Great Commission.

In addition to bringing together the church planters, the Holy Spirit was instrumental in bringing together those who would help the church to develop. Among these were Barnabas and Saul. Barnabas was sent by the Jerusalem church (Acts 11:22). His ministry would, undoubtedly, strengthen the new converts in the "apostles' doctrines." Saul also contributed. We must not overlook, however, that this was also a training period for Barnabas and Saul as they were to be sent within a year on the mission to the Gentiles. That multi-cultural environment in Antioch was, no doubt, ideal as a training ground for these cross-cultural missionaries.

The Holy Spirit sent church planters from Antioch. It is important to note that even though Barnabas had been a member of the church in Jerusalem for seven years, the matter of his commissioning for missionary service was not referred to that church. The Antioch congregation, functioning as a full-fledged church, confirmed what the Holy Spirit instructed it to do: "*Set apart for Me Barnabas and Saul for the work to which I have called them*" (Acts 13:2). The Bible then affirms that: "*Then when they had fasted and prayed and laid hands on them, they sent them away* (v.3).

In examining the birth of the Jerusalem Fellowship and the establishment of the Antioch Congregation, we find several lessons that are important for us today as we design church planting strategies.

- The Holy Spirit gave birth to the Jerusalem Church. The Church in Antioch was also started through the initiative of the Holy Spirit.

- The Apostles and later others who were converted (e.g., Barnabas, Paul) were instrumental in

11

establishing a sound doctrinal foundation (teaching that which the Lord had commanded).

- The Jerusalem Church became an "enabler" in the establishment of the Church in Antioch. Although the Church in Antioch was never referred to as a "daughter congregation" it can be established that the Jerusalem Church was an enabler in that out of it came some of those who started and later contributed to the development of the Antioch Church. The Antioch Church, in turn, served a similar function in relation to the churches which Paul and Barnabas started.

- The Jerusalem Church and the Antioch Church became sister churches with the latter contributing financially when the former was in need.

The accounts of these two churches can be very useful in helping new Christians learn how the believers gathered to carry out the functions of a church and how a church can be involved in fulfilling the Great Commission including starting new churches. In the final chapter of this book we have included the experiences of these two churches in a story format.

Paul's Church Planting Methodology

In his book, *Planting Churches Cross-Culturally,* David Hesselgrave describes what he calls the "Pauline Cycle" of church planting.[33] He suggests the following outline:[34]

Missionaries Commissioned (Acts 13:1-4)

At Antioch, while the church fasted and prayed, the Holy Spirit instructed them to *"Set apart for me Barnabas and Saul, to do the work to which I have called them"* (Acts 13:2).

It was not the church that called the missionaries nor was it the church that motivated them to go. The church merely recognized the fact that the Holy Spirit had already called them for missionary service. The task of the church was to merely release them to do the task that they had been assigned. We see here, once again, the Holy Spirit as the initiator in the church planting endeavors. There is a sense in which we can say that the Antioch church "enabled the church planting team." They did so by providing the training ground in which the church planters could sharpen their skills for cross-cultural church planting. The church also enabled them by providing an on-going prayer and moral support for the church planters while they were starting churches in distant places. The Antioch Church, therefore, was more of a "sending church" or an "enabling church" than a "mother church" to the new churches which were springing up all over Asia Minor.

Audience Contacted (13:14-16; 4:1)

During the early part of his church planting ministry, Paul made it a custom to go first to the Jewish Synagogue in the target city. There he generally found three types of people: (1) Jews; (2) Proselytes; (3) God-fearers. In most instances the bulk of those who received the message were from the last two categories. When the Jews shut the doors of the synagogue, Paul simply looked for other places in which to meet (e.g., the Hall of Tyrannous) and kept right on with the task of finding those who would listen to the gospel.

Today one of the challenges we face is gaining a hearing among a people who are presently satisfied with their religion and lostness as we understand it. Contacting an audience may start with finding a person of peace in a home, in the work place, or wherever they might be.

Gospel Communicated (13:17 ff.; 16:31)

Paul employed a wide variety of methods to communicate the Gospel. He preached in the synagogues, taught in rented halls, proclaimed in palaces (during his trial), witnessed by the riverside, evangelized in homes, led people to Christ in jails, shared Christ in the market place, communicated the gospel in stadiums, employed his contacts as a tent-maker to reach people with the gospel (Priscilla and Aquila) and even used the experiences of being mobbed and shipwrecked to let people know the good news of the Gospel.

If Paul were alive today he would undoubtedly use all the means at his disposal (including the fax, electronic mail, tele-conferencing, blogs, etc.) to proclaim the message of Jesus Christ. As Paul proclaimed the gospel to those who were previously excluded from the family of God (Gentiles and outcasts) he insisted that these new believers would be first class citizens in the Kingdom of God (Ephesians 2). We face today the challenge of helping people t understand they are sinners in need of forgiveness and salvation through storying.

Hearers Converted (13:48; 16:14, 15)

Paul took the Great Commission seriously. His goal was not merely the proclamation of the Gospel but the conversion of the hearers in order that they might begin to live a life of Christian discipleship. Leading people to make a decision to receive Christ is the primary goal of CBS. From the very beginning of the CBS process, this objective must guide everything the Bible storyer does. Some people will make a decision to receive Christ much sooner than others. While in some instances much patience and persistence will be required, the goal remains the same.

Believers Congregated (13:43)

Paul was aware that in order to disciple the converts adequately he needed to gather them together in congregations. These congregations met in rented halls, homes, and wherever space was available. The important consideration was not the place but the congregation of believers. We find no instance in which Paul took into consideration the place in which the congregation was meeting in order to determine if this group could be considered a church. As a matter of fact, Paul repeatedly used the expression "*the church which is in your house*" (Rom. 16:5; 1 Cor. 16:19).

Current CBS strategies need to give a high priority to the matter of establishing the church community to exist among a people, grow, and reproduce itself in a continuing cycle. The process must not fall short of starting churches. Ebbie Smith affirms this when he states:

> The ultimate goals of Church Growth in the 21st century seek to stimulate and help Churches and churches increase in SIZE and STRENGTH at the same time they increase in HEALTH and SERVICE and all these elements of growth remain in balance.[35]

Faith Confirmed (14:21, 22; 15:41)

As Paul and his missionary team saw people come to a saving knowledge of Christ, they immediately proceeded to make plans to disciple them. *"Paul and Barnabas preached the Good News in Derbe and won many disciples. Then they went back to Lystra, to Iconium, and on to Antioch in Pisidia. They strengthened the believers and encouraged then to remain true to the faith"* (Acts 14:21, 22). In this account, we perceive in his ministry and in that of ministry other Apostles as well a strong commitment to provide a strong foundation (the teachings of Christ) for the emerging churches.

In CBS, the Discipleship Track has been designed with the purpose of confirming the faith of the new believers. Every storying ministry must emphasize this need for maturing believers along with the imperative of bringing people to faith.

Leaders Consecrated (14:23)

"In each church they appointed elders..." (14:23a). It is significant to take notice of the fact that they called each of these congregations "a church." The appointment of elders in each of these young struggling churches points to the fact that Paul and his fellow church planters fully expected these congregations to become strong, responsible, reproducing churches. Their appointment of elders was a statement of faith as well as a practical step to ensure that these churches had the leadership they needed to attain their full potential. In order for reproducibility to take place and for churches to be started CBS efforts must focus on discovering and training leaders.

Believers Commended (14:23; 16:40)

"And with prayer and fasting they commended them to the Lord, in whom they had put their trust" (14:23b).

The believers were placed in the hands of the Lord and not of the "sending church." While it would be important for them to know that fellow Christians cared for them, the new congregations were put in a direct line with their maker "the Lord," to whom they were to go in times of need and persecution. This practice implies trust in the Holy Spirit as well as in the new believers and their newly appointed leaders.

Could it be possible that if we show paternalism (the trait of treating converts as children and not respecting them as believers) toward new Christians and new congregations we are also showing paternalism toward the Holy Spirit? Could this type of attitude imply that the Holy Spirit is not able to lead and undergird these churches in their early stages of development? Paul and his fellow church planters saw themselves as enablers (midwives) in the process of allowing the life of Christ flow to the new believers, thus, giving birth to these new churches.

A key component in CBS is that of placing the leaders in the hands of the Lord and entrusting them with the responsibility of continuing the evangelistic and church planting efforts in their local communities. The act requires faith on the part of the church planter but in order for reproduction to take place, the Bible storyer must have an exit strategy.[36] By exit strategy we mean a plan for the missionary to withdraw and allow the new congregation to serve in its own strength.

Relationships Continued (15:36; 18:23)

Some time later Paul said to Barnabas, *"Let us go back and visit our brothers in every town where we preached the word of the Lord, and let us find out how they are getting along"* (15:36). Significantly, Paul and Barnabas had a deep and abiding concern for the welfare of those whom they had led to the Lord. It is also significant to note that they did not call them "children" but "brothers." We see here a concern that seeks to enable the continued spiritual growth of new Christians but also respects knowing that in the ultimate analysis they belong to the Lord and not to us.

As we employ CBS methodologies we need to find ways to encourage those whom we have trained without creating a spirit of paternalism on our part or dependence on theirs. Bible storyers should seek the spiritual maturity of the new Christians.

Sending Churches Convened

The question of whether Gentiles needed to become Jews culturally and ceremonially in order to be considered fully Christian was of crucial importance to the church. Had the Christian movement imposed upon the Gentiles the practices of the Judaizers, Christianity would have remained a sect of Judaism. One local congregation could not settle this question alone. We do not see the Jerusalem Church summoning the other churches as though she had a higher status than the others. The fact that the Antioch Church sent Paul and Barnabas (a former member of the Jerusalem Church) indicates that there was a degree of autonomy which each of these churches enjoyed yet a sense of colleagueship as sister churches. Acts 15:2 appears to indicate that it was the Antioch Church that took the initiative in this matter.

Due to political, social, and religious realities, churches will relate to other churches differently in various cultural settings. Certainly, we want to encourage and support the churches that emerge from our CBS efforts. We need, however, to be careful not to impose upon them ecclesiastical administrative patterns or social traditions that are foreign to their setting.

This outline suggested by Hesselgrave is useful in whatever church planting methodology the church employs. Those employing Bible Storying methodologies will be well advised to pay attention to the steps that Paul and his team members followed. In order for churches to be started, church planters need to be sent, audiences need to be contacted, the gospel needs to be communicated, believers need to be congregated, their faith needs to be confirmed, local leaders need to be consecrated, and believers need to be commended.

These phases of the church planting process, however, need to be applied differently in different cultural settings. For example, audiences are contacted differently among different people groups. The manner in which people congregate will vary in the different settings. This applies to the manner in which the local groups will relate to one another.

While the application of these phases will be different, having an idea of what needs to take place in order for

17

churches to be started will be useful. In other words, if Bible storyers have this or a similar pattern for their work, they will have a clear sense of direction and will have a good understanding of the manner in which they need to utilize the Bible Storying process to accomplish their church planting goals.

A firm and strong biblical foundation is essential to effective church planting in whatever method of church starting the initiator employs. The Bible remains the foremost guide.

A Harvest Theology

Church planting storyers need to be driven by a clear harvest theology. Harvest theology teaches that conversion and new churches make up the essence of Christian missions. Caring for people remains important but must not override the goals of conversion and church starting. Such a theology enables church planting storyers to distinguish between the activities that minister to people as ends in themselves and the activities that are clearly focused on leading people to an experience of salvation in Christ and to the formation of churches where new believers can grow in their faith and practice.

Donald McGavran, the founder of the modern church planting movement, made it very clear that a harvest theology was essential to the implementation of the Great Commission. He explained:

> Up to this point, mission had been widely defined as "God's total program for man...." Mission may be defined much more meaningfully. Since God as revealed in the Bible has assigned the highest priority to bring men into living relationship to Jesus Christ, we may define mission narrowly as **an enterprise devoted to proclaiming the Good News of Jesus Christ and to persuade men to become His disciples and dependable members of His Church**. Even after establishing the priorities among "good deeds," social action, and evangelism, the Church still has many baffling alternatives, and this defini-

tion is necessary if we are to discover among them the path desired by the God Who Finds.[37]

To bolster his argument that Christian missionaries should be motivated and guided by a harvest theology, McGavran mentions the fact that Jesus sent the laborers unto the harvest, that the parables of Jesus emphasized an actual finding, and that God himself is a searching, saving God.[38]

Most Evangelical missionaries (among them many who are committed to Bible Storying) are not motivated by a social gospel that merely seeks to minister to human needs. We are committed to focusing clearly on leading people to Christ and encouraging them to gather into reproducing congregations.[39] As Dr. Ebbie Smith points out in his book, Growing Healthy Churches, *"Christians and churches should proclaim the gospel by word and deed."*[40] Several benefits can be derived from a harvest theology:

- A harvest theology enables us to focus clearly and intentionally on leading people to an experience of salvation in Jesus Christ as soon as they are ready to make an informed decision. This emphasis does not mean that we are to pressure people to accept Christ before they know what they are doing or have a desire in their hearts to do so. As a matter of fact, one of the benefits of the Chronological Bible Storying approach is that it goes to great pains to ensure that people have a sufficient understanding of the basic Bible truths to know clearly what they are doing when they make a decision to become followers of Jesus Christ.

- A harvest theology enables us to make a distinction between the storying strategies that focus on leading people to Christ and forming them into congregations and those that concentrate only on their personal spiritual development. There is a sense in which all of the tracks proposed by CBS trainers (evangelism, discipleship, church planting, leadership training) are important. Having a harvest theology, however, will enable the storyer to establish priorities in the CBS process.

- A harvest theology helps us maintain a sense of urgency in guiding people to experience salvation in Christ. There is a sense in which there must be a tension between sharing sufficient information with the people and leading them to the point of deciding for Christ. This tension must be maintained if we are to avoid the pitfall of becoming too complacent in the implementation of our storying strategies.

- A harvest theology keeps us from making the mistake of seeing a storying methodology as an end in itself instead of a means to the goal of leading people to Christ. CBS is merely a tool in the hands of church planters to reach oral communicators in ways that other approaches do not. The church planting goals must be established at the very beginning and the methodologies for accomplishing the goals will then need to be designed.

- A harvest theology causes us to be more sensitive to the work of the Holy Spirit in order that we might discern what he is doing in the lives of the people in our ministry focus group. We do not suggest or imply in this segment of the book that these characteristics that we have described above are totally lacking in many of the storyers that are currently working on the field. Instead, it is our intention to focus on these so that there will be a greater degree of awareness and a deeper commitment on the part of storyers to a harvest theology that leads to the initiation of countless numbers of churches among the various people groups around the world.

A harvest theology is absolutely indispensable if churches are going to be started in connection with Bible storying methodologies. There must be a clear focus in the mind of the storyer on bringing people to a conversion experience. This focus, however, must be balanced with a commitment to follow through with effective discipleship. As Keith Stamps states: "Care must be taken that 'Harvest' theology not place an undue emphasis on the speed of harvesting to the extent that it later laments the back door and still born believers."[41]

A Vision for Church Planting

Along with a firm biblical foundation and a certain harvest theology, Church planters must have a compelling vision for the new churches. Having a compelling vision for church planting is absolutely essential if the efforts of a Bible storyer are going to result in the establishment of churches.[42] The Bible states categorically *"without vision, the people perish"* (Prov. 29:18). It is clear in Scripture that the persons who made the greatest impact for the kingdom of God were driven by a vision.[43] In the Old Testament we have the inspiring example of Nehemiah who led the people of God to reconstruct the wall around the city of Jerusalem:

- Nehemiah became aware of the need (1:1-4).

- He sought a vision from God (1:4) by fasting and praying (v. 5), interceding for the people (v. 6-10), and asking for God's blessing (v. 11).

- He caught a vision and was willing to sacrifice to attain it (2:1-10).

- He shared the vision with the people (2:18).

- He developed a strategy which demanded unity and cooperation to fulfill the vision (4:15-23).

- He worked to overcome internal and external obstacles in order to attain the vision (5:1 - 6:1-4).

In the New Testament we find evidence that Paul's life was driven by a clear and compelling vision. In 2 Tim. 2:11, Paul states: *"And of this gospel I was appointed a herald and an apostle and a teacher."* The book of Acts gives detailed accounts of the way in which Paul implemented his church planting vision. In 2 Cor. 11:24-27, Paul gives an account of the struggles he encountered in fulfilling his vision. In Acts 26:19 Paul testifies to the fact that he was not disobedient to this heavenly vision.

Vision is an absolutely essential element in the life and ministry of effective church planters. As we study the experiences of those who have planted thriving, reproducing congregations where others thought it was impossible, we invariably conclude that these church planters were motivated and guided by a clear, compelling vision of what God wanted them to do.

George Barna defines vision for ministry as: **"a clear mental image of a preferable future imparted by God to His chosen servants and is based upon an accurate understanding of God, self and circumstances."**[44] From this definition one can conclude that vision is clear, is preferable to the current state, concentrates on the future, is given by God, is a gift to leaders, is tailored to circumstances, reflects a realistic perspective, is dreaming the most possible dream, and is built on reality.[45] From Barna's definition of vision we can develop the following list of characteristics of a compelling vision.

- Church planters must have an end result view. They must be able to form a mental picture of the end product, the church that God wants them to start. God told Abraham to "look up in the heavens and count the stars - if indeed you can count them." Then he said to him, *"So shall your offspring be"* (Gen. 15:5). God wanted Abraham to picture himself as the father of a mighty nation.[46] This picture would be his guiding light throughout his entire pilgrimage.

- Church planters must have a futuristic view. The picture is not of what is but what can be with God's power. This implies that the church planter will lay aside all physical, mental, and emotional obstacles and will see the vision from the perspective of God's infinite power.

- Church planters must have a compelling picture. Because God has given the vision, it carries with it the profound motivation to bring it to fruition. It is not a matter of personal accomplishment but a matter of obedience to God. Paul stated: *"I was not disobedient to the vision from heaven"* (Acts 26:19).

A question that prospective church planters often ask is "how can I catch a clear and compelling vision?" The first thing that needs to be said in response to this question is that catching a vision is the result of a process. This process involves several important phases.

- The church planter should spend time studying the Bible to have a clear concept of God's redemptive purpose. There must be not only an understanding of passages such as Matt. 28:19, 20 but a burning desire to reach people with the gospel of Jesus Christ. God will not give a vision to someone who does not have a deep commitment to implement it.

- The church planter should spend time in continued prayer and reflection. This prayer should seek God's will for the church planter's life, a specific commission from God, a clear understanding of the ministry focus group, discernment regarding the type of church planting team that is needed, and a clear picture of the type and size church that God wants to establish in that place.

- The church planter should gain first-hand acquaintance with the needs and opportunities pertaining to the ministry focus group. Personal acquaintance with the values, lifestyles, needs, and attitudes of the ministry focus group can help the church planter develop a culturally relevant vision of the strategy that is needed to start a church among that group and its potential for growth and reproduction.

- The church planter needs to dialogue with other vision-driven church planters to get input from them in an effort to fine tune the vision. Others who have developed and implemented a church planting vision can help the church planter gain a clearer concept of what the vision is and how it can be formulated and realized in a culturally relevant manner.

- The church planter needs to articulate the vision. This in itself will involve a brainstorming type process that begins with writing down all of the ideas that come to mind as the church planter prays and meditates. These ideas can then be organized into categories for the purpose of selection and evaluation. This process can lead to the formation of a core group of ideas that can serve as the foundation for the subsequent development of a "statement of purpose, values,

23

strategy, target group, place of ministry, and finances."[47]

The next step will be the formulation of the vision statement. In order to ensure that this statement is effective in communicating the vision, the following questions need to be asked: "Is the vision clear? Is it challenging in the sense that it inspires to action? Does it create mental pictures? Is it future-oriented? Is it both realistic and stretching? Is it culturally relevant?"[48]

Bible Storyers must have a clear vision for church planting if their efforts are going to result in the establishment of churches. We cannot expect Bible Storying efforts to automatically result in churches if from the start a clear harvest theology and the compelling vision are not present in the hearts of the storyers. Stated differently, church planters who employ CBS methodologies can be very effective in starting churches. Conversely, Bible storyers who utilize this approach as an end in itself will seldom see churches result from their efforts.

A Knowledge of Church Planting Models

A fourth factor need by church planters who desire to use storying is a working knowledge of church planting models. In light of the fact that church planters who employ storying are needed in many different settings in urban as well as rural areas around the world, a wide variety of church planting models are needed. It is very likely that among un-reached people groups house church models will be needed. On the other hand, in many urban areas there may already be some churches in existence which need to be challenged to help start churches among oral learners. Due to the fact that books such as *Starting Reproducing Congregations* have extensive discussions on the variety of models it is not necessary for us to discuss all the models or to present lengthy descriptions of these models.[49] Instead what we will do is select some of the models that might be more compatible with the settings where Bible storying is likely to be employed as a strategy for starting churches. In this segment, therefore, we are going to discuss pioneering, parenting, partnering, propagating, and training models.

Pioneering Models

The main feature of pioneering models lies in the fact that the church planter has to start from scratch. Due to the fact that this model does not have a sponsoring church, the church planter cannot count on a church planting team, financial resources, or hands-on guidance. The church planter, therefore, does not inherit a core group but has to recruit one. By the same token, the church planter does not have a ready-made church planting team but has to develop one generally from the new field in which the new church is being started. Some of these potential disadvantages, however, may actually become advantages:

- The new congregation can be fashioned in a way that reflects the biblical priorities of the church planter over against traditional approaches that perhaps were effective in the past but are less relevant today.

- The new congregation will almost automatically be contextualized in its community because that is where the members have come from.

- The new congregation can develop in such a way that it will be a part of its genetic makeup to reproduce itself.

- This model provides unlimited opportunities for church planters who have excellent self-starting capabilities.[50]

Parenting Models

Parenting models are those in which a Mother (or Sponsoring) church assumes the responsibility of starting a daughter congregation. In this model the resources of members, finances, guidance, and facilities are made available to the daughter congregation. In this model the mother church sends a core group to new community to start a new congregation. This model has several advantages.

- First, the new congregation has leaders for its ministries from the very beginning.

- Second, the new congregation has a financial base from which to work. As this core group tithes, it provides the financial resources that are needed to start the congregation.

- Third, the leaders of the new congregation have a solid doctrinal foundation from the start.

- Fourth, the core group has a strong connection with the mother church and there is on-going support for the new congregation.

While many potential advantages stem from using this model, in an oral learning setting this model could have many disadvantages unless measures are taken to adapt the methodology that is employed. For example, if the people from the core group are literate and want to impose a literate methodology upon the new believers who are oral learners, the resulting situation may seriously undermine the church planting efforts.

The only way that a parenting model might be effective in an oral-learning setting is if the church members that are selected are trained in oral learning methodologies and make a solid commitment to utilize and support them as the churches are being started. For example, some members of a literate church receive extensive training in communicating with oral learners and in utilizing storying methods. In addition to this they are willing to be involved in the initial evangelization efforts but are then willing to help train oral learners for positions of leadership so that the new church will be in a position to reach, disciple, and train oral learners.

Partnering Models

There are several ways in which the partnering model can be employed. One of the ways is for an existing literate church to assist an oral-communicator's church to be established. Another is for an oral-communicator's church to help a literate church start a ministry or a ministry or a church among oral-communicators. Still another way may be for an oral-communicators church and a literate church to partner in starting an oral-communicators church in a new community. Yet another way in which a partnering church could help would be to encourage some of its members (of the literate church) to receive training in Bible Storying and to assist in reaching and disciple oral learners utilizing this methodology. Throughout the process, however, it must be kept in mind that the goal is not literacy but to reach people in whatever stage of orality they might be. If literacy does eventually occur as a result of this effort, that will be wonderful. Care, however, must be taken not to limit the number of people that are reached with the gospel message and the number of churches that are started because of implicit or explicit literacy standards that are set by the Bible storyer.

Propagating Models

In most oral learning settings, propagating models provide the best options for starting reproducing congregations. Among the propagating models we would note multiplication through leadership training and multiplication through church planting movements.

Multiplication Through Leadership Training

One of these models accomplishes the goal of church multiplication by establishing a network of cell groups through theological education and evangelism by extension. Designed by George Paterson while a missionary in Honduras, this model strives for "the voluntary multiplication of a church of any size by God's power, in daughter churches of cells that, in turn, plant granddaughters and so forth."[51] This program integrates church planting with discipleship. From the start, an effort is made to teach converts the full meaning of discipleship. This strategy, according to Paterson, involves commitment to obey the specific commands of Jesus before and above all else.

These commands are to: "1) Repent, believe, and receive the Holy Spirit; 2) Be baptized; 3) Love God and neighbor; 4) Break bread; 5) Pray; 6) Give; 7) Disciple others."[52] By setting up a large number of Theological Extension Centers and a leadership structure that oversees and encourages church starting efforts, Paterson has saw more than a

27

hundred churches started in the part of Honduras where he served.

Claylan Coursey in Malindi, Kenya developed another example of church multiplication through leadership training.[53] After concluding that *"the primary responsibility for church planting belongs to individual believers banded together as a local church,"* Coursey designed a plan to help pastors train their church members to start churches. The training involves eight simple steps:

- Select a New Work Committee for the church;
- Select the area for the new work;
- Prepare the sponsoring church;
- Prepare the selected area;
- Begin the infant church;
- Teach the new church about finances;
- Plan with the new church its facilities;
- Dedicate the new church[54]

By training the pastors and having on-going follow-up sessions, Coursey was able to see over ninety new congregations started in Malindi in three years.

Several distinctive features of the Multiplication through Leadership Training Model are evident:

- Every Christian is seen as a potential church starter.
- Training is tied in with implementation. Paterson, for example, added an "Evangelism" course to Theological Education by Extension. He did not feel that simply educating leaders without involving them in church starting ministries was enough.
- The leadership structure is designed to ensure the continuity of the church planting efforts.
- Obedience to the commands of Christ is expected. Paterson states: *"Basically, church multiplication comes from our love for Christ and the resulting desire to obey his commands to disciple all peoples or ethnic groups."*[55]

While it is obvious that this model works well in rural areas among people in the lower socio-economic levels, people like Richard Scoggins, Paterson's colleague, have found it useful among urban, educated, affluent, middle-class Americans in the shadow of the oldest Baptist church and the oldest synagogue in the United States (in Providence and Newport, Rhode Island.[56]

In the past both of these models have been used predominantly with literate or partially literate people. However, the methodology that is employed could very well be adapted to oral learners in many parts of the world.

Multiplication through Church Planting Movements

Another means to gain church multiplication through storying relates to the strategy of church planting movements. David Garrison defines a church planting movement as a rapid multiplication of indigenous church that plant other churches and experiences a movement that sweeps through a people group or population segment. [57] In the history of Christianity perhaps two of the most effective developers of church planting movements have been the Apostle Paul and John Wesley. Through their leadership they sparked multitudes of new congregations. A review of the leadership of the Apostle Paul reveals that there were several principles which he followed in his church planting efforts.

- Paul was sensitive to the leadership of the Holy Spirit who instructed him where not to go as well as where to go (Acts 16:9).

- Paul was willing to pay the price to go where God wanted him to go even if it meant suffering for Christ (2 Cor. 6:5).

- Paul was willing to adapt himself to the target group to whom the Lord sent him (1 Cor. 9:19-23).

- Paul was willing to adapt the presentation of the gospel to each target group (compare Acts 13 with Acts 17).

- Paul saw himself primarily as a church planter. He did not stay long in any of the places where he started churches.

- Paul did not tie his strategy to the availability of buildings. When he was no longer welcome in the synagogues he moved to whatever was available such as schools (Acts 19:9), homes (Acts Col. 4:15), market place (Acts 17:17).

- Paul was willing to trust the leaders that emerged in each church plant (Acts 14:23).

- Paul was committed to training and trusting the leaders (Acts 14:21; 15:35);

- Paul did everything he could to encourage the leaders (Acts 14:22). In so doing he was instrumental in spawning a church planting movement that impacted the world.

Several observations can be made regarding church planting movements.

- These movements generally develop along the lines of people groups instead of simple geographical configurations. This means that these movements quite often cross national and political boundaries.[58]

- If a church planting movement is going to succeed, lay people will of necessity play an active role in starting new congregations.

- Even though church planting movements appear to be totally spontaneous, structure is needed to continue to inspire and to train locally those who will start new units.

- Many church planting movements are taking place in societies that are basically pre-literate. Outreach methodologies, therefore, need to employ narrative formats (e.g., Storying) rather than literate formats.[59]

- Some of the church planting movements are utilizing the "bolder forms of contextualization" when it comes to establishing culturally relevant congregations.

Timothy Tennent explains: *"Whether we are talking about Jesus Mosques in Bangladesh or Christian Sannyasins in India or Sokagakkai styled discussions and discipleship groups in Japan, new ideas are being promoted today in ways we haven't seen on this scale before."*[60]

- Church planting movements only take place when indigenous leaders who experientially know the heart language and customs of the people do church planting.[61]

Commenting about the impact of indigenous leadership in the church in China, Raymond Fung states:

Perhaps the single most obvious conclusion about Christianity in China today is that it is Chinese. People in the streets and in the communes no longer see Christianity in China as a foreign religion. Now after some 25 years of isolation, and eight years of acute suffering, with zero visibility, the church is seen to have survived and grown. For the first time in its history, the church has won its right to exist in China as a Chinese church. For the first time in its existence, it has its roots in Chinese soil.[62]

Multiplication Through Cell Churches

Cell Churches generally are congregations that meet for worship and celebration together but carry out most other church functions in small groups that meet in facilities other than the church meeting place. These Cell groups typically have between 5 and 20 members. They utilize lay-led cells with highly trained top leadership. The ordinances are not carried out in the cells but in the central congregation during the celebration services. Leadership support is carried out in two levels with the lay-leaders supporting themselves and the upper-level leadership being paid by the church. Celebration typically takes place in the central congregation on Sundays.

The cell church usually requires a pastor who is a strong leader and a visionary who can communicate his vision. Training for all levels of leadership takes place weekly.

Discipleship also takes place in the cells during the week. Usually, cell churches do not have a Sunday School program. Their goal is to multiply to the limit of their structural support.

Evangelism, koinonia, and accountability take place in small groups. The control of these cells is from the top down. ***The most appropriate analogy for reproduction in this model is that of an Octopus – if you cut an arm off, it will grow it back.*** Leadership rises from within and is rarely brought in from the outside. The Cell Church model utilizes a highly organized structure. The Cell-based approach helps in seeking to narrow the back door of the church. The offerings are typically used for staff salaries, facilities, programs and mission offerings and projects.[63]

Multiplication through Basic Churches

Basic Churches are much like cell groups in Cell group churches with the exception that they are not usually part of a larger congregation. The basic churches are independent, self-governing, and self-propagating entities. The basic church model includes simple churches, house churches, and other types of churches that function as small groups. As Rad Zdero points out, a significant part of the ministry was carried out in homes. He explains:

> The gospels report that homes – among other places- were a natural part of Jesus' life and ministry. Christ was worshipped as a baby in a house (Matt 2:11), he healed Peter's mother in law at home (Mat 8:14-16), the Last Supper was held in a house (Mat 16:18), and Jesus preached to people crowded in homes (Mark 2:1). Christ also trained his disciples during a hands-on assignment by sending them out in pairs to preach from village to village. They were instructed to find a man of peace in each village that was responsive to their message and build a spiritual base of operations from that home (Luke 10:1-10).[64]

Zdero adds that the apostle Paul utilized a house church strategy to reach many with the gospel of Jesus Christ such as Lydia in Philippi (Acts 16:14-15, 29-34, Believers - Troas (20:6-8,20) and in other places where he often used the expression "*the church that meets in your house*" (Rom 16:3-5 [Priscilla and Aquila]; 1 Cor. 16:19 [Priscilla and Aquila]; Col 4:15-16 [Nymphas]; Philem. 1:2. [Philemon)[65]

The basic church model is usually made up of 5 to 20 members (sometimes up to 50 or 100).[66] The leadership comes from laypersons. There are no highly trained leaders in the basic churches themselves although the trainers of the leaders (e.g., Strategy Coordinators, Strategic Catalyzers) are generally highly trained. A strategy coordinator is a worker who assumes responsibility for developing and implementing a comprehensive strategy that partners with the whole body of Christ to bring an entire people group to faith in Jesus Christ.[67] The ordinances are carried out in the local group. The leaders of basic churches are self-supported. Celebration may be intermittent in some cases. In others, however, there are no joint celebrations and no paid facilities.

The local basic churches do not have strong central leaders. Training is required and may occur weekly, monthly, or quarterly. Usually basic churches do not have typical, graded Sunday Schools. Evangelism, *koinonia*, and accountability occur in small groups. Control of basic churches is typically diffused although most of them are a part of local, regional, and national networks. ***The most appropriate analogy for the reproduction in this basic church model is that of a Starfish: You can cut off any part of the fish and it will grow a whole new starfish.*** In basic churches leadership rises from within. The structure consists of independent units, yet in network with one another. This approach is very effective in helping to close the "back door" of the church. The offerings are used for local ministry and outreach.[68]

Cell churches as well as house churches are the two types of churches that are contributing the most toward church planting movements. David Garrison explains:

> Church buildings do appear in Church Planting Movements. However, the vast majority of the churches continue to be small reproducible cell

churches of 10-30 members meeting in homes or storefronts... House churches may look the same as cell churches, but, they generally are not organized under a single authority of hierarchy of authorities. As autonomous units, house churches may lack the unifying structure of cell churches, but they are typically more dynamic. Each has its advantages. Cell groups are easier to shape and guide toward doctrinal conformity while house churches are less vulnerable to suppression by a hostile government. Both types of churches are common in Church Planting Movements, often appearing in the same movement.[69]

Multiplication Through Training for Trainers

Another model of church planting through church multiplication is Training for Trainers (hence T4T). It has been described as a very simple way of evangelizing, discipling, and training leaders. The assumption is that just about anybody who is willing can do it. T4T has resulted in tens of thousands of new churches in Asia. This methodology that is being adapted and utilized in many parts of the world is producing astonishing results. One of its strongest points is that T4T leads people from the beginning to develop the habit of putting into practice what they are learning. Another one of its strengths is that each person who finishes and applies the materials immediately starts another group. This leads to the multiplication of believers, disciples, and leaders. T4T has been adapted from materials developed in Asia.

Stephen Smith and W. Mark Snowden developed the Oral-Preference Learners' version of T4T.[70] In light of the fact that these training materials can be obtained separately it is not our intention to duplicate them here. Instead we will highlight the adaptations that have been made so that T4T can be an effective tool for oral-preference learners.

The first two sessions of T4T entitled "Kingdom Connections (Evangelistic Portion)" are focused on giving trainers a vision to reach out to their circle of influence. After spending time on a memory verse (2 Tim. 2:2) and

34

reviewing the goal, the trainers tell the story of Peter's visit with Cornelius. This study is followed by a post-story dialog that has the purpose of helping the trainees understand and apply the story. The second session involves modeling of witnessing experiences and reviewing the process with the trainees.

The next segment of T4T includes four sessions entitled "Trainers Evangelize Circle of Influence." In the first three sessions the following stories are told: The Creation and Fall; The Ten Commandments and Golden Calf; The Sacrifice for Sins & Jesus. Each of these stories is followed by dialog. In the final session the trainers share personal testimonies.

The next segment of T4T for oral preference learners consists of three confirmation sessions entitled: "Trainers Firm Up The Believers' Decision To Follow Christ And Form Them Into A Church." These sessions use the following format: Worship, Story, Review, Verse to Memorize, Obedience Testimony (relating a mini story), Review, and Trainer Follow-up. In these lessons the following stories are told: The Good Shepherd; Jesus Calls His Followers; and Coming of the Holy Spirit and the First Church.

The final section of T4T for Oral-Preference Learners entitled "Staying Connected to God (Discipleship Section) consists of "8 Boxes or Chests." These are: 1) Walk; 2) New Birth; 3) Faith, Hope, and Love; 4) Submit; 5) The Gospel; 6) One Body, One Head; 7) Put off the old, Put on the new; 8) Stand. Each of these lessons is geared at helping the trainees to learn: 1) a Bible story; 2) a name for the Chest/area; 3) a picture to draw to remember it; 4) a verse to memorize, and 5) a specific way to obey.

As one reviews this Training for Trainers (Oral Version) it is clear that the people who adapted this material were most specific about two goals. First, they wanted to make sure that they communicated the biblical concepts that are essential to evangelism, discipleship, church starting, and leadership training. The second goal was to make the effort to employ oral strategies to communicate the biblical concepts. One of the challenges of employing this approach is to continue to equip oral learners so reproduction will occur. Another one is that of continuing to take steps to avert moving to a literate model which could undermine the initial purpose for using this approach.

Combination of Approaches

It is quite natural for someone committed to a particular approach to believe that it is not only the best approach but also the only approach that should be utilized. Equally natural is the feeling by those employing the CBS strategy to feel a keen sense of commitment and loyalty to this approach. In numerous instances a storyer will have the luxury of implementing and utilizing a CBS strategy without opposition or interference. In these situations the storyer will be faced with settings in which there are very few believers and there is not a tradition among the people that would encourage resistance.

Often, however, there will be a Christian witness and some form of ecclesiastical tradition that has been embraced by the people either directly or indirectly. In these situations the utilization of some of the features of existing methodologies may actually enhance church planting efforts in a given setting. Lovejoy describes this type of combination of approaches:

> Currently we have some field personnel who are combining Bible storying with other approaches. Essentially they are keeping other frameworks or methods but using Bible stories as the scriptural content in place of proof texts from the epistles. TRT as a storying version of T4T is an example of this happening. So is the preaching in established, traditional churches where pastors have incorporated heavy use of Bible stories in their sermons.[71]

The T4T adapted by Stephen Smith and Mark Snowden has the potential of being a very valuable tool for church planting among oral learners.[72] The fact that it has been adapted for oral learners avoids possible pitfalls that could undermine storying efforts.[73]

Another example of a combination of approaches it that of establishing agricultural training centers and utilizing

Chronological Bible Storying in an evangelistic and church planting strategy. Lovejoy describes one of these approaches:

> People studying the Philippines situation say that nationals using CBS to plant churches were almost always those who had studied CBS at the agricultural training center. The pattern was that new churches sent a member to the Agricultural/CBS training for weeks or months and he then went and planted a church, which in turn sent someone to the Agricultural/CBS training, etc. Churches did not train their own members to do CBS and church planting.[74]

A similar approach is being used in Dhaka, Bangladesh, as is evident in the following report:

> A fourth group of agriculture trainees has received Bible storying training during a two month stay at the training center near Dhaka. Three previous groups were from tribal areas. The latest group is from a Hindu background. In addition to learning the stories so they can retell them, the men are learning to explore what happened in each story, what did God or Jesus do, what lesson they learn from the story, and the characteristics of God or Jesus they find in the story. Reports from previous groups show the men are using the stories where they live.[75]

Perhaps one of the greatest challenges Bible storyers face is found in areas where literate and oral learners live in close proximity with one another. While on the one hand it is necessary for Bible storyers to employ methodologies that reach oral learners, it may be necessary on the other hand to employ parallel tracks for literates. An intransigent attitude may alienate people and create barriers. Steven King expresses this concern when he states:

> We have to face the fact that in many groups there will be an unrelenting pressure to move

BIBLE STORYING FOR CHURCH PLANTING

toward a literate approach. I believe we must develop narrative models that respect both at the same time. If we fail to do this we will be seen as an enemy to the common good and our precious vision will be discarded.[76]

Keith Stamps also believes that there are settings in which a combination of communication methods needs to be employed due to the characteristics of the people in a given area. He explains:

Preaching with Bible stories must be encouraged in order to help break down the barriers among those who are not acquainted with this form of preaching. Story clusters must be presented to help train leaders to deal with the issues their church faces. It is helpful to combine Bible stories and a memory verse that completes the doctrinal issue being taught.[77]

Ken Sorrell who is working in some settings in Latin America where literate local Christians who live in close proximity with oral learners have already established the strong traditions also expresses this concern. Sorrell explains:

There are instances in which a balance between Storying and more literate methodologies are needed in light of the challenges and complexities of the part of the world in which we serve. I have yet to find anyone's model of church planting to be effective in its purest sense. Some level of adjustment has always been needed and has proven to bring a greater level of effectiveness when these adjustments have been recognized and implemented.[78]

Based on his observation of evangelization efforts in Latin America, Sorrell has concluded that there are numerous instances in which even literate people will benefit from utilizing oral methods to gain a gain a better understanding of the Scriptures. He states:

38

When I reflect on our evangelistic efforts one of the first thoughts that come to my mind is not where on the continuum between Storying and literate strategies do we implement in our work, but how do we better prepare our national partners and leaders to feed off of and interpret Scripture from Scripture alone. Even when leaders move to a more a literate level in their abilities, few will ever be able to fully take advantage of their newly acquired skills in terms or accessing volumes of resources or commentaries that will allow them a broader perspective of hermeneutics. Yes, a few will, but the greater majority will not. This fact alone will inform our decisions as to where Storying and other narrative strategies are need while still be [being] fully aware of the literate issues as well.[79]

Paul F. Koehler also stresses the importance of equipping storyers to employ a variety of strategies especially in areas where there is great cultural diversity. He believes that storyers should not assume that in every instance they are going to work with a single people group with strong cultural distinctives. He explains:

In many places today a more realistic picture is that of a mosaic of different cultures overlaid on top of one another in geographical proximity. This is certainly true nearly everywhere in India, and also in many urban contexts around the world. Thus a storyteller should be prepared to tell an appropriate Bible story to a person from any cultural background.[80]

This perhaps points to the fact that more advanced training is needed to equip those who need to utilize a variety of approaches to reach and equip the people in the culturally pluralistic urban areas of the world.

It is also important for those who have received training to realize that there are instances in which

CBS is not a standalone church planting tool.[81] Among the ways in which CBS is being used in combination with other ministries we find the following:

- Point of Ministry (Situational Storying)
- Service Ministries Storying
- Relief Ministries Storying
- Development Projects Ministry Storying
- Evangelist and Pastor Training
- Small Ministry Group Training
- Teach it, Tell It Method
- Bible Storying Camps
- Cooperative Training Projects
- Public Storying Lecture Presentations
- Personal Evangelistic Presentations
- Short Term Mission Ministries
- Bible Story Websites and "Blogs"[82]

In order for Bible storying to be an effective tool for church planting, appropriate models need to be employed. The Bible storying methodology may be flawless yet if the appropriate church planting model is not employed new believers are not going to be encouraged to gather themselves into congregations and to seek to be instrumental in starting other congregations.

The models that have been presented here do not represent an exhaustive list. Our primary intention is to encourage Bible storyers to find the type of church planting models that will be instrumental in reaching, discipling, and challenging large numbers of believers to reach their people group for Christ, gather them into congregations, and continue to reproduce themselves. J.O. Terry has learned from experience that many different types of churches are needed. He explains:

> There are many different types of churches that are being planted around the world. We

have many different examples of church planting going on. One young storyer in Chandighar, India, has had as many as five storying groups going at one time, all leading into worship groups. Church does not always look the same. One group of ladies was in a sewing class and paused for stories from the Word, worship and prayer. Some were only family groups with or without extended family. Some were occasional churches that met when there was opportunity--like the older rural churches here in America that had worship whenever the preacher was in town. Yet the group exhibited the fellowship in the Spirit and bond of love that characterized the Acts church. Storying church planters need to take into account the cultural characteristics of the local group in determining the type of church that needs to be planted.[83]

A Purposeful Plan

Another factor that enables Bible storyers to be effective as church planters is the possession of a purposeful plan. Lovejoy alludes to this when he describes the church planting that took place in the Philippines during the time that Jim Slack was utilizing CBS strategies. Lovejoy explains.

That use of CBS took place in a responsive area which was very ready to move into church life. But they also had a very purposeful plan of leading new believers into becoming a church. They were focused on church planting and shaped what they did all along the way to that end. (I fear that our typical CBS training has lacked this intense focus on Church Planting. When have we ever modeled 5-10 stories from Acts so they could see how we foster biblical ecclesiology in a new group?) They went from the resurrection/ascension stories straight into Acts without a pause. They were very

41

intentional about using dialog questions that led people to identify themselves as followers of Jesus who by all rights should be functioning as a church. They then asked new believers to act in obedience to the stories as church members ought. Story by story they sought to inculcate the habits of life that would lead to reproduction. Salvation, as important as it is, was not their goal. Planting reproducing churches was the goal.[84]

It is very likely that in this case there was a combination of a receptive society and a purposeful plan to gather the believers into churches very early in the storying process. It is indeed wonderful when there is a convergence of factors that facilitate the commitment to new congregations. In some settings, however, church planting will not take place in the early stages of Bible storying. In some of these settings there may be a strong opposition to the gospel or even persecution. Despite this, however, when there is a purposeful plan to start churches, somehow people who are touched by the Spirit of God find a way to meet (in homes or other places) and to begin to function as a body of believers. ***What is sad is that there may be some settings in which people are ready to begin to function as a body of believers but the Bible storyers either do not have the sensitivity to detect this or the skills to enable it.***

Keith Stamps also calls for having a purposeful plan in the utilization of storying methodologies. He states:

"Where do we go from here?" This is the question that many new storyers have. Some CBS teachers recommend that after cycling through a well crafted evangelistic series one cycles through it again asking questions of obedience and characterization. If you go farther, generally an Acts set is proposed with Epistle teaching slotted in... In order to avoid this confusion some of the options that can be explored are: 1) developing a leadership training track very early in the process; and 2) giving the storyers in training a larger list of variations on storying that cover all areas of traditional and "simple" church practice so that the first option when hitting a bump in the road is not necessarily to revert to a literate approach.[85]

Whether one follows precisely what Stamps is suggesting or not, the point that needs to be made is that a purposeful plan must be in place to guide the storyers in a direct line toward starting churches through their CBS methodologies. Some of the earlier storying tracts must be seen as preparatory phases to the church planting tacks. ***Actually the seeds for church planting need to be sown from the very beginning of the Bible Storying process***. If the storyers do not have such a plan from the inception they may wander without a sense of direction. This purposeful plan should include: A Willingness to Retell Stories; Sticking to the Fundamentals; Avoiding Literate Overhang; and An Unwavering Commitment.

Willingness to Retell Stories

A factor in a purposeful plan that contributes significantly to effectiveness in the utilization of Bible Storying is the ability and willingness on the part of the storyer to share the story as many times as might be necessary. Charles Madinger emphasizes the importance of repetition in the utilization of oral strategies. He states:

> Orality works when its message demands repetition. One motif in successful programs is "I listened again and again." Listeners receive the message through entertainment education with participatory forms for learners to engage at deeper mental and emotional levels that lead to volitional responses.[86]

Jeremy Taliaferro has found that repetition is essential in the people groups among whom he and his team have been starting churches. He explains:

> We have had missionaries tell us that storying does not work in their environment. Upon further investigation of the situation we have found that storying has not worked due to the

practices and mistakes of the missionaries rather than CBS as a methodology. Generally the problem lies in the retelling of the story. Westerners do not feel comfortable with telling and re-telling the story 3, 5 or 7 times (whatever is necessary for the hearers to learn or memorize the story). They generally feel uncomfortable with asking them to retell it over, because it seems offensive to say "you don't have it yet, let's try again." It is really difficult to train storyers to realize that repetition is important and most oral cultures do not find it offensive at all. We have found that if the people hear the story once or twice and never learn it in their heart, the rest of the process falls apart. For instance they will only be able to answer surface questions, but when they have memorized the story they know the details without thinking about it, they have internalized it and can answer more profound and spiritual questions. I would say this is the biggest problem with storying on the field today.[87]

As Taliaferro points out, repeatedly retelling the story enables the people not only to internalize it more effectively but also to understand the deeper implications more readily. Like Taliaferro, James Brandt has found that retelling can be a very important part of the training process in Nepal. He states:

During the ten-day workshop I had opportunity to present 46 Bible stories in an overview of the Old Testament. What a joy for this administrator to be once again telling Bible stories to a group of eager students! My overriding goal was to equip my students to teach the story of the gospel as presented in the Old Testament when they returned home.

Next I placed students into small groups where one student would retell the story. It was encouraging to see members of the groups listening intently and helping one another retell lessons from God's Word. Each session concluded with one individual retelling the story to the entire class of approximately 50 students.[88]

As Brandt points out, retelling should not be confined to the Bible storyer in training sessions. Encouraging new believers to retell the stories they have heard is a very important part of the Bible Storying strategy. From South Asia we have received the following report:

> One woman from the H people heard a story from God's Word for the first time. The next day, she was telling it to her friend. Then the day after that, she was gathering a few people to hear the story. In just a few days, she was gathering large groups and telling them the story that she had heard![89]

Working with Mayan cultures Ed Beach is constantly reminded of the crucial role that repetition plays in the Bible storying process. He asserts:

> Oral cultures often use repetition in ways that are very different than we would. For instance, insufficient repetition may be intended to cast doubt whereas what we would think of as undue repetition may be reinforcing what is true or what is a main point. One time a North American coworker went through one of our trainee's stories and methodically cut out all the repetition. In doing so, she completely ruined the proper telling of the story and left it difficult to understand from the hearers' point of view.
>
> Regarding these issues of information flow rate and repetition, the word for "slowly" and "do it well" are the same word (kyeb'a' or similar equivalents) in many Mayan languages. The idea is that if something is done well then it is done slowly. And if it is done slowly then it is

done well. That's a tough one for outsiders to come to grips with! 90

In addition to this, Beach points out that there are other benefits to the use of planned repetition in the use of Bible stories. He explains:

> Storyers also need to keep in mind that repeated elements not only tie a story together but may have other intentional uses such as highlighting a character's prominence or giving significance to some event or other story element---all of which needs to be intentional and done with understanding or risk possible misunderstanding. [91]

Adhering to the Fundamentals

Still another element in a purposeful plan for effective storying for church planting relates to adhering to the fundamentals. The story is told that when Vince Lombardi became the coach of the Green Bay Packers he started his first meeting with the team by holding an object in his hand and saying: "This is a football." The moral of the story was that the coach sent a message from the very beginning that he was going to emphasize the fundamentals of the game of football.

As we have sought to discover why some Bible Storying efforts have not led to the establishment of churches in some areas, one of the truths that have become obvious is that often the storyers have not put into practice the fundamental principles of Chronological Bible Storying. Some have said: "We have tried CBS but it has not worked." When we have asked for more details we have discovered that in some instances the person doing the Bible storying did not follow even some of the most basic CBS steps. Among these are:

- **Identify** the Biblical Principle that you want to communicate – simply and clearly.

- **Evaluate** the worldview issues of the chosen people group.

- **Consider** worldview – the bridges, barriers and gaps.

- **Select** the Bible stories that are needed to communicate the biblical principle

- **Plan** (craft) the story and plan the dialog that is going to follow the story, focusing on the task to be accomplished.

- **Communicate** the story in a culturally appropriate way, using narrative, song, dance, object lessons and other forms.

- **Apply** the principle by facilitating dialogue with the group, helping them to discover the meaning and application of the story to their own lives.

- **Obey** the discovered principle by implementation steps to be taken by the individuals.

- **Accountability** – establish accountability between group members by mutual and reciprocal commitments to implement the Biblical principle in the conduct of their personal lives between members of the group, their families, and other personal relationships.

- **Reproduce** – encourage the group to reproduce the Biblical principle, first by demonstrating the principle in their own "witness of life" then in sharing the principle with others.[92]

In light of the fact that excellent books have been written on this subject, we will not deal with all of the CBS principles here but will refer the reader to these resources.[93]

Avoiding Literate Overhang

In anthropological literature the term "culture overhang" means that people automatically (and unconsciously) carry with them their own cultural understandings and communicational patterns and seek to impose them upon a people group of a different culture.[94] In Bible Storying this happens when literates, who do not understand primary oral learners, treat them as if they were literates. Literate overhang, therefore, means that Bible storyers employ literate means in their attempt to reach and disciple primary oral communicators. One of the ways in which this "overhand" expresses itself is by focusing on imparting concepts without making provision for their application. LaNette Thompson shares an analysis of the type of Bible Storying that has this weakness. She states:

> It primarily consists of head knowledge – discovering truths. New believers accept these truths. We have been remiss in helping them to understand that discipleship goes beyond understanding truths to developing a relationship with the living God.[95]

In his book, *Communication of the Gospel to Illiterates*, H.R. Weber points out in a dramatic fashion the fact that literates need to understand and utilize the communication methods that oral learners employ. Prior to focusing on Weber's statements we need to point out that he reflects the culture of his day in the utilization of the word "illiterate." For a number of reasons we now prefer the term "oral communicator."[96] Describing himself as a "Western Theologian," he observes:

> The more intimately the Western theologian came to know them, the more he was amazed at their powerful imagination, their ability to see: pictures, actions and significant happenings in nature and human life. Many of these illiterates revealed themselves as true artists in observation and communication... Thus very soon a great change came about. The Western theologian who had come to teach became a pupil. The longer he who had come as a literate among illiterates lived with these 'letter-blind' people, the more he realized that he himself was blind among those who could see; that he was a stunted poor intellectual with only *one* means of communication (through pallid abstract ideas) among imaginative artists who thought and spoke in colorful, glowing pictures, and symbols.[97]

Avoiding literate overhang, therefore, involves more than simply developing an appreciation for the socio-cultural characteristics of a group of oral communicators. It requires an understanding of and identification with oral learners to the extent that we are able to utilize their communication means with ease and effectiveness. Could this be called: "communicational incarnation?" Was this what Paul had in mind when he spoke of becoming "all things to all people" (1 Cor. 9:19-23)?

Weber explains what needs to be done in order for this incarnation to take place:

> What we must realize anew, however, is that the manifold wealth of the Biblical message cannot be understood and communicated merely through the intellect and through words. The book of God's revelation, with its witness to Christ which has come down to us in human language, points to a person and to a story – with all the varied nuances and aspects of personal and community life. It is the task of the Church to transmit to the world this life of Christ and this story of salvation; through the Church the world is to share in this abundant life and in this redemptive history... We must learn, and use the illiterate's methods of communication... The church is called upon to re-examine not only the contents but also the form of its proclamation of the Gospel in worship, in teaching and in missionary encounter.[98]

Perhaps at the heart of the issue of communicating with oral learners is the perception (hopefully not prejudice) on the part of literates that the former are simply not equipped to understand the gospel message. H. R. Weber addresses this issue when he states:

> The evangelization of illiterates, as of all others, requires as its primary concern that there shall be a full encounter with the living Christ at the earliest possible moment; this is the real missionary encounter. Such an

encounter in its fullest involves a communication of the full Biblical message including its dogmatic elements, to the illiterates. Is this full encounter impossible without first making the illiterates literate? It has never, to my knowledge, been said in so many words that before becoming a Christian a man must become literate. Nevertheless, the possible over-emphasis on literacy at this stage has certain dangers. It seems to share the cultural fallacy of the modern world, the emphasis on word-culture, to which we have already drawn attention. There is a real danger that it will delay a primary Christian experience which is available to illiterates and literates alike.[99]

An Unwavering Commitment

If churches are going to result from storying efforts, the Bible Storyer must be an unwavering commitment to doing whatever it takes to accomplish the task. Jeremy Taliaferro stresses the need for commitment when he states:

We have seen people who have tried to use storying but are not ready to commit to it exclusively. When it becomes difficult or demanding they tend to return to traditional methods that they have used previously and are more comfortable with. We believe that storying can be used successfully in any culture, oral or otherwise. Mostly because it is so flexible, you can mold it to the culture.[100]

Keith Stamps echoes this when he states:

People need to understand that Bible storying is a discipline that requires effort, exercise and patience. For some it may be as easy as falling off a log. For many it is much harder than picking up a printed lesson and working through its outline five minutes before "show time.[101]

50

Stamps has learned from personal experience as a storyer and a trainer of storyers that without effort, exercise, and patience storying endeavors will not lead to church planting. There are many things that can happen in the life of the storyer as well as in the lives of the hearers that will discourage or sidetrack church planting efforts.

J.O. Terry affirms Taliaferro's and Stamp's emphasis on commitment and persistence. He explains:

> Had I not persisted, just accepting failure of the form of early Chronological Bible Teaching, I would have moved on to something else. But by persisting I was able to puzzle out what made things work and how to adapt the teaching for the people I worked with. By persistence I was able to learn from my own trial and error (especially in the beginning) and by learning from the folks I worked with (my interpreters) and the folks I worked among (listening to them and observing how they did things). Instead, I see the whole Bible storying process as a three dimensional process that has depth as we learn cultures, orality, and andragogy methodology. [102]

Failure was very important as a learning tool. First it was instructive for me to find out what worked and what did not work and, hopefully, why it did or didn't work. That way I could make intelligent choices and adaptation. Second, it was very important for me to fail first so that those I was training did not have to fail and become ashamed. Then there is a third reason for persistence which has to do with delayed response or fruit. As I mentioned earlier, persistence paid off in Bangladesh. It also happened in Orissa where Calvin Fox harvested some of the crop I had planted years before.

So if we quit too soon, then we abandon growing seed whose time has not yet come. I still maintain that we never go wrong by sowing the Word of God. We don't know who is being touched by the Word. Also if we are not persistent, then those we work with (local nationals) will not be persistent. So we cannot always control church planting and when it will occur. We want it to happen and we work persistently to make it happen.[103]

Conclusion

We started this chapter by stating that Bible Storying does not take place in a vacuum. An individual's knowledge, personality, vision, and theology greatly influence the storying process, especially if such an effort is going to result in church planting. We then stated that church planting storyers need to be driven by a harvest theology. Such a theology enables church planting storyers to distinguish between the activities that minister to people as ends in themselves and the activities that are clearly focused on leading people to an experience of salvation in Christ and to the formation of churches where new believers can grow in their faith and practice.

We also stated that having a clear vision for church planting is absolutely essential if the efforts of a Bible storyer are going to result in the establishment of churches. We also affirmed that in light of the fact that storying church planters are needed in many different settings in urban as well as rural areas around the world, a wide variety of church planting models are needed. These include pioneering, parenting, partnering, and propagating models.

Another essential tool that church planting storyers need is knowledge of the available tools to train those who will be leaders in the churches that are started. As an example of a very effective tool, we have briefly described the version of T4T Training for Trainers that is specifically designed for oral learners. We cannot over emphasize the fact that the storyer plays a crucial role in reaching people with the gospel and gathering them into biblically sound, growing congregations. This should motivate the storyer to continue to gain knowledge and develop skills to be truly effective in the challenging but rewarding task.

Also, Bible storyers need to avoid "literate overhang" if they are to be effective communicators. An underlying factor in all of this is the storyer's unwavering commitment to start churches. Practitioners view this as an indispensable trait for storyers who want to be effective church planting. The chart in appendix A can help in assessing the equipment of a Bible storyer who wants to be an effective church planter. **_The bottom line is that storyers need to be equipped if their efforts are going to result in church planting._**

Much of what is said of the training storyers coming from outside the target culture need to be effective does not necessarily apply to storyers who are already members of the target group. There is a sense in which they will instinctively know what to do due to the fact that they are full participants in the culture of their group. This segment, therefore, is not a model for training insiders but for training the outsiders who need to be to learn the worldview, culture, and communication patterns of their target group.

Having reviewed the equipment storyers need for effective church planters we now turn our attention to the important issue of understanding the cultural setting of the ministry focus group.

Chapter 2:
Understanding the Setting

We are using the Bible as the source, but carefully selecting stories and choosing key terms that will give the best opportunity possible for these people to understand and receive the gospel in their own cultural context.

Tom Dyson

We believe that storying can be used successfully in any culture, oral or otherwise. Mostly because it is so flexible, you can mold it to the culture.

Jeremy Taliaferro

Understanding the cultural context of a people group or population segment is an absolute necessity if Bible storying efforts are going to result in the establishment of indigenous churches among people groups and population segments. Simply taking a method or strategy that has worked well in another setting and attempting to apply it without any modification or adaptation is a guaranteed recipe for failure. An understanding of the cultural setting of a ministry focus group (people group) requires: 1) a worldview analysis of the ministry focus group; 2) a study of their communal worship patterns, and 3) an assessment of the level and function of orality.

Understanding the Worldview

A worldview analysis is a detailed description of the way people within an ethno-linguistic people group or homogenous unit act, think, believe, live, and function.[104] It consists of the central assumptions, concepts, and premises shared by the members of a culture or subculture. In light of the fact that worldview is at the center of a people group's culture it influences all of the group's subsystems (social, religious, political, economic, linguistic and technological). Worldview is so engrained in the hearts and minds of individuals within a people group that it is impossible to achieve their spiritual transformation without an understanding of the way they believe, think, act, and live. Dr. Jim Slack stresses the importance of studying a people group's worldview before evangelizing and starting churches in their context. He makes three valuable observations:

- In order to engage and seek to lead individuals from any non-Christian worldview to consider and embrace a Christian worldview, evangelists should first identify that person's worldview and key on it as the biblical teachings are applied to their worldview. One should engage and address specific worldview issues in the presentation of biblical truth to be effective and relevant in communication with those being evangelized.

- Persons contacted with generic non-worldview specific Christian presentations are seldom effectively engaged and changed, much less impacted.

- The bottom line for Christian evangelizers, church planters and disciplers is that they must identify the worldview of the persons and people they are going to engage, evangelize, and disciple according to the Scriptures (the Great Commission). If the evangelizers do not act in conformity with the worldview analysis, ritualistic, syncretistic, ineffective Christian lives will result. This is what Paul said on many occasions, even when he said he must be a Jew to the Jews and a Gentile (*ta ethne*) to each of the "*ta ethne*."[105]

For the Bible Storyer, an understanding of a people's worldview is absolutely essential. To the degree that a people's worldview is identified, and to the degree that those items contradictory to Christianity are addressed in the communication of the Gospel, to that degree syncretism will be hindered from entering the lives of the believers and the Gospel will usually be seen as relevant to them.

Some very important benefits, therefore, can be derived from studying a people group's worldview. Among these are:

- Locating and understanding the ethnographic center or core of the target people.

- Discovering "bridges" within the culture, or similarities between the target culture and Christianity that can serve as points of contact

- Discovering "barriers" within the culture that must be addressed as the Gospel is communicated

- Avoiding syncretism

- Determining what biblical truths (core beliefs) a people group needs to understand in order to receive Christ

- Selecting the Bible stories that best communicate these core beliefs

Knowing how many of the core beliefs people already have in their worldview can be helpful in determining how much time to spend in reviewing, clarifying, correcting, and strengthening what they already know and how much to focus on what they do not know or understand. (See appendix D) The experience of Philip with the Ethiopian Official is an example of this procedure. Even though Luke may not have included the entire conversation it is quite likely that the Ethiopian already knew the first fourteen of these core beliefs. He was a God-fearer if not a proselyte into the Jewish faith. He had gone to Jerusalem to worship. He was reading from the book of Isaiah. His question related to the identity of the Suffering Servant whom Isaiah had described in this passage. It is very instructive that the Bible says: *"So Philip began at this place in the Scriptures and explained the good news about Jesus"* (Acts 8:35).

Philip's initial conversation with this official led him to conclude that he did not have to start with the story of creation with him. He already knew that. In light of the fact that the official already understood enough of the Jewish Worldview (See appendix E), he could start with the New Testament and share with him the story of Jesus.

There is a sense in which working with people who have a Roman Catholic background makes it possible to move more rapidly through the Old Testament stories and into the story of Jesus. Many Roman Catholics already know that God is the creator of the universe, that Jesus is the Son of God (born of the virgin Mary), and even that Jesus died on the cross. If, however, they have not studied the Bible and come to a personal experience of salvation in Jesus Christ there are some very important Bible teachings that they do not know (See appendix F). Some of these teachings are that salvation is found in Jesus Christ alone, that Jesus is the only mediator, and that they can be sure of their salvation.[106]

Like Philip, therefore, we can start with the stories of Jesus when we are working with a people group that has a Roman Catholic background. This principle does not mean that the Old Testament stories are not important. These stories can be taught at the appropriate time (perhaps in the discipleship phase) or even interjected if necessary. It does mean that there are some groups with whom the storying process can move much more rapidly and among whom churches can be started much sooner than with other groups.

Jim Slack, who was involved in the use of CBS in the Philippines where many churches were planted, observed that this was a responsive area that was very ready to move into church life.[107] The people in this area had a Roman Catholic background and therefore already had a desire to learn more about God, Jesus, the Holy Spirit, the Church, and the other doctrines found in New Testament stories. The religious background of this people group made it possible for the storyers to move more rapidly to the New Testament stories and to focus on church planting earlier than what might have been the case among people groups of other religious backgrounds. People groups who already have some sort of Christian background may have notions about the church that need to be addressed in the discipleship phase.

Christy Brawner used a limited set of Matthew stories among the *favela* dwellers in the slums of Brazil. In light of the fact that the people had some familiarity with Christianity and perhaps a copy of the New Testament, Christy chose to use The Gospel According to Matthew because it was the first book and easy to find. She selected all seven lessons from this same book.[108] A second set of story lessons also was taken from Matthew's Gospel.[109]

Situations in which the people have some background in Bible knowledge often indicate the advisability of the "Jesus First, Genesis Second," that is, beginning with the stories of Jesus. This approach immediately takes advantage of interest and openness. The storyer can then return to Genesis and the Old Testament stories as part of the discipling process.

With people who have an Islamic worldview (See appendix G) there is generally more of a need to spend a good bit of time helping them to gain an understanding of the character and actions of the God of the Bible as well as of the person and mission of Jesus. The evangelist must be willing and able to explain many misconceptions the Muslim may hold about the Christian view of God and the nature of Jesus.

Many people in the world today hold a basically traditional religion or animistic worldview. These people often believe in a Creator God who made the world and then left it to itself. Many animists believe that there is a Creator God but feel that that God for some reason got angry with human beings and turned his back on them. They feel that this God is the most supreme in a hierarchy of gods but these lesser gods as well as the evil spirits that can aid them and that they need to appease with their sacrifices and rituals. They look to magic persons (shaman) to help with problems.

With these people groups that hold an animistic worldview, storyers may need to spend more time sharing Old Testament stories to set a foundation for the stories of Jesus. It is obvious that with these types of people groups there is more of a need to start with the story of creation. In some cases even before that with the story of how evil spirits came to be. The experience of Paul and Barnabas in Lystra (Acts 14) is an example of an animistic group that totally misunderstood Paul's message and the meaning of the miracle that took place right before their eyes (See appendix H, Animistic Worldview).

Peoples, who are marginalized from their society, especially tribal peoples living among Hindus with their caste system, have a strong desire to find acceptance and identity outside the caste identity. A witness that promises that desired acceptance and identity has immediate appeal. Such a result was achieved when during storying among the Kui people of India a conversation like the one recorded below occurred between one of the older listeners and the storyer:

> I had told the Creation Story with Adam and Eve followed by the Flood Story and the command that God gave to Noah's sons and their wives to have children to replenish the population on earth. Following the Tower of Babel Story during a tea break an older man approached and spoke to me through interpreter: "I am hearing that Adam was the first man. Later when all the wicked people died and only Noah and his sons remained, Noah became the grandfather of all the people. So I'm hearing that Noah is my grandfather (ancestor). Is Noah your grandfather, too?" "Yes," I replied, "he is my grandfather, too." Then the man said, "If Noah is my grandfather, and Noah is your grandfather, then we are brothers!" "That's true," I replied, "We are indeed brothers." "Well, if that's true it is wonderful news because I am somebody, like you! I want to be a Christian so we can all be brothers." I assured the man that our story was not yet finished and soon he would hear more stories telling how we can also be brothers and sisters in the Family of God. The man added, "We don't want to become Hindus and not be accepted as brothers. We want to be Christians!"[110]

In some situations, people who would normally be resistant to the Gospel have been drawn to Christ through miracles. There have been incidences of many who have been healed through prayer by visiting evangelists. Others who were suffering from demonic bondage have been freed. In these cases, the people know the Jesus of healing and the Jesus of deliverance, but do not know the Jesus of salvation. A situation like this existed some years ago in Nepal where Indian evangelists visiting the country were involved in healing and deliverance, leaving behind many people who were open to know more about Jesus. In situations like these it is more productive to go directly to the stories of Jesus to evangelize and plant a church, and later to return to the background Old Testament stories as part of discipling and maturing the new believers in their faith. Church planting can take place rapidly among people groups of resistant religious backgrounds even without miracles. There are instances in which there appears to be a special visitation of the Holy Spirit and people, even from resistant groups, have become receptive much sooner than anyone expected.

Missionaries like Tom Dyson, serving in Oaxaca, Mexico, take the time to learn the worldview of their people group and take this understanding into account in designing their storying strategies. He explains:

> We are still meeting with only unbelievers at this point. We have carefully chosen and crafted Bible stories that we pray will lead these people to salvation. You might wonder why we have to produce stories when you can find Bible stories anywhere. We are working to make these stories understandable to the particular culture that we are working in. We are using the Bible as the source, but carefully selecting stories and choosing key terms that will give the best opportunity possible for these people to understand and receive the gospel in their own cultural context.[111]

We cannot over emphasize the fact that an analysis of the worldview of a people group is absolutely essential for effective Bible storying. One of the real values that should come out of the worldview studies prior to storying is a better understanding of the better ways to a reach people with the gospel, disciple them, and lead them to start churches in its community. Among the questions that need to be explored are: Why do a people worship? Remember, this information about their worldview is their situation before they become believers. This understanding of worldview reflects their past worship habits. When do they worship? Where do they worship? What makes a place holy and acceptable for worship? Who can join in worship? Who leads worship? What is their worship practice or ritual?[112] An excellent tool for tool for constructing a worldview was developed by Drs. Jim Slack and Lewis Myers and appears in their manual, *To The Edge*. Since have done an excellent job of explaining what worldview is and how one can attain information about the worldview of a people group or population segment, have limited our discussion of this important topic. We recommend that Bible storyers become thoroughly familiar with this manual.[113] J.O. Terry has developed a very practical tool that he calls "Discovering Worldview Issues and Processing World View Information." Because it is so useful we have included it in Appendix K.

Understanding Communal Worship Patterns

Along with an understanding of the worldview of the population segment, Bible storyers must also seek to comprehend the communal worship patterns of the group. Cultural understandings regarding communal worship and worthy leadership directly influence church planting that takes place in connection with Bible Storying. Those who are not used to trusting non-family members or who do not normally worship communally may be resistant to moving from storying group to church. Peoples who have more experience with communal types of worship may be more open to new congregations.

Muslims, for example, already have some practice of communal worship as they gather weekly for prayers and teaching. They are, however, suspicious of those outside their immediate acquaintance or family. Filipinos with their Catholic tradition worship out of devotion, especially of their personal saints, and have a concept of communal worship. Meeting together for worship and interacting as a church body are different however. Hindus, who come from a background of individual devotion or worship of deities in the context of need or petition, are reluctant to gather together. Many animists do their worship and rituals out of fear to keep the spirits and their potential harm at bay. They may individually seek some shrine or natural location to make an offering and petition to the inhabiting spirit for some boon or blessing but usually worship as families or clans. These perceptions regarding communal worship among the various cultural groups may influence their receptivity to the idea of meeting together or trusting others outside their families and can impact the pace of church planting among them.

The place in which worship takes place is also a factor in church starting. Many Hindus, for example, want a "holy place" to conduct their worship. Some castes of urban Hindus do not like to worship in homes because they are not holy places because people do "dirty" things there. Places of worship may also need to accommodate cultural practices of separate seating for men and women or even in some cases different castes. In one area in Karnataka State in India, a man wanted to begin a church in his home which he shared with a Hindu brother. The brother, however, rigorously opposed sharing his home with the Christian God. The result was extensive family strife.

Muslims need to face a certain direction when praying. Many of the tribal people are comfortable with a shaded place or some shelter. But they more readily follow a "spiritually powerful person," such as a shaman (witch-doctor) and various intercessors, who were their spiritual leaders before conversion. Some of the *jamats* (small Muslim worship groups) in one South Asian country frequently moved because of persecution and fear of betrayal by nonbelievers attending the worship. Worshipers only knew each other by given name and not family name in the event of betrayal. In African contexts, there has been difficulty in starting house churches because women can be accused of immorality if they spend too much time in the courtyard of a man who is not their husband, even if the man's wife is present. Rivalry between clans can also inhibit church growth.

Issues surrounding support of church leaders vary worldwide. Among some Asians a teacher or leader does not do menial work. Bi-vocational leaders may have difficulty finding adequate support. In many places where there is a predominance of Roman Catholics, they may not be accustomed to tithing in order to help support their leader. It is crucial to teach them biblical stewardship principles. They will give an offering (viewed as alms) once in a while but they are not accustomed to systematic giving to support the local congregation. The church planter must look for innovative ways to encourage local support. Among the Kui in India, worshipers bring farm produce and chickens to be auctioned off at the close of the worship time for their offerings. In Central America some years ago church members were encouraged to have a garden of which a portion of the produce was to be their "tithe."

Former agricultural missionary Calvin Fox encouraged pastors in India to be good farmers, first to feed their families, as a prerequisite to being good pastors. He called them "farmer-pastors." Income is very low in that region and this provided a workable solution to support.

The concept that people have of what a church should be often influences their response to the idea of starting a church. Speaking about the receptivity of their people group in Africa to church starting efforts, Thora Broyles states:

> We are in an environment which knows something of church. We are not in a completely virgin environment. The students in the [CBS] program have come out with a capacity to apply the Word of God that goes beyond most of their seminary-trained counterparts. This has resulted in churches that are truly growing in spiritual growth. And in fact a comment I made to David, my husband, about 6 months ago is very apropos. I said: "In places where there are no churches people do not know how to transition from a story group to a church. And therefore when the stories end no one seems to know where to go from here."[114]

In situations such as this it is imperative that the church planter introduces the concept of church to the storying group as soon as possible and provides clear instructions on church formation, guiding the group through the process.

Understanding the Level and Function of Orality

Along with the knowledge of a people group's worldview and the patterns of communal worship among them, the Bible storyer should develop a clear understanding of the level and function of orality in their setting.[115] Several areas need to be analyzed to provide a good foundation for effective church planting. These include:

- Ascertaining the storying history of your people group. Do people share stories (often heritage stories) with each other (in groups) on a regular basis? If there is already a history for this practice, people typically respond more readily to our storying efforts. If that is not the case, it will take longer to get the storying process going and to help people to become comfortable with it (See appendix B).

- Assessing the people group's experience with group participation. How often do individuals participate in group discussions? If the individuals in a people group have had significant experience participating in group learning and discussion sessions, they will respond more readily in Bible Storying efforts. If the opposite of this is true, it will take longer to get people to feel comfortable participating in group discussion. Among some people groups there is such a high regard for "the teacher" that they feel that any question or comment on their part would undermine the teacher's authority and credibility. These factors need to be taken into account in designing storying strategies (See appendix B).

- Ascertaining the implications of gender participation in discussion groups. Do some groups divide discussion segments by gender? Are there some situations, for instance, in which women would not speak if men are present in the discussion group? If that is the case, would it be the better part of wisdom to divide the group by gender segments in order to ensure that all of the people in the storying sessions feel comfortable enough to participate in the discussion? Are there instances in which this division may be helpful initially but can be reversed with time and as the group progresses toward becoming a congregation?

- Ascertaining the mental retention capacity of oral communicators. As they are being trained, Bible storyers are at times told that oral learners have an amazing capacity to hear, internalize, retain, and repeat the stories they hear. One of the reasons for this is that oral communicators realize that they will only carry with them that which they can internalize. It must be pointed out however, that not all oral communicators have the same mental retention capacity. Some may have a much stronger tradition for story-telling than others. It is important, therefore, for Bible storyers to ascertain just how much mental retention capacity those in a particular people group have. Not taking this into account could well result in overwhelming the oral communicators. Because oral communicators must remember all they need to know, they can be selective in what they remember. In addition, many oral communicators may live in an environment where very little new happens so there is little need or pressure to learn aggressively (See appendix B).

- Ascertaining the amount of material that needs to be shared. How many stories can those in a particular people group retain and reproduce? If the Bible storyer does not address this question it could well be that overloading a people group with an inordinate number of stories will contribute to a lack of reproducibility. LaNette Thompson expresses this concern when she states:

  Although we encourage the hearers to repeat the stories, unless special training is involved or the stories are placed on cassettes, new believers cannot easily reproduce the entire storying track.[116]

Ascertaining the mental retention capacity of the individuals in your people group is essential in designing church planting strategies through Bible storying. The mental retention capacity varies widely between oral groups. This very likely is related to the storying history of the people group. Generally the more experience people have with storying, the higher their mental retention capacity will be. If a storyer discovers that the target people group has very limited mental retention capacity, the storying strategy should include opportunities for repetition of the stories (See appendix B). This strategy can also be supplemented with the use of other resources such as cassettes, videos, voice boxes, etc (See appendix L).

Orality/storying assessment can help the storyer to have a better understanding of the target people group and to design appropriate stories and methodologies to increase effectiveness.

Conclusion

An understanding or the cultural context in which Bible storying will take place is absolutely essential if such efforts are to be effective in reaching people with the gospel message, discipling them and gathering them into congregations. Some of the things that contribute to this understanding are analyses of the worldview, communal worship patterns, and orality /storying experience. For a tool to assess the level of cultural understanding on the part of the Bible storyer see appendix C.

Chapter 3:
Developing the Strategies

My hunch is that the solution to the "getting to church" issue lies in a combination of more intentionality, better training with materials that fully equip personnel to make the transition from believers to church, and more follow up to see that it actually happens.

Grant Lovejoy

We have tried to break the training into small groups so that it would model what house church could/should look like. We have the story training create the atmosphere of small group integrating storying, prayer time, worship, and going outside of the class to put it into practice.

Donald Barger

Many churches are being started with Bible Storying strategies among oral communicators throughout the world. In an effort to learn how we can be even more effective in church starting we have interviewed and corresponded with Bible storyers in different regions or the world. Based on the information we received we compiled a number of factors that contribute to effective church planting. These factors, therefore, are presented with the purpose of stimulating further thought and dialog as well as encouraging Bible storyers to be more focused and more intentional in ensuring that their Bible storying efforts result in the establishment of many churches among the people groups with whom they are working. These factors include initial strategies, church starting strategies, training strategies, continuity strategies, and depending on the Holy Spirit.

Initial Strategies

The strategies that are employed to contact a people group, share Bible stories, lead people to faith in Christ, disciple them, and gather them into worshipping congregations are crucial if Bible storyers are going to be effective church planters. These strategies must be characterized by adaptability in the presentation of the stories.

Adaptability on the part of the Bible storyer is absolutely essential if such efforts are to result in church starting. This adaptability must address the presentation of the stories, the number of stories that are utilized, the story sets that are employed, the place in which people meet, and the methodology that is employed.

Adaptability Regarding Presentation

Adapting the presentation of the story to the level of understanding of an individual or a people group is an essential element in the communication of the gospel message. In his book, *The Great Physician*, G. Campbell Morgan states that Jesus adapted the presentation of the message of salvation to the individuals whom he addressed. Morgan explains:

> Here we summarize briefly by saying that we never find our Lord dealing with two different persons in exactly the same way... To Andrew and John He said, "What do you seek?" To Simon He said, "You shall be Rock." To Philip He said, "Follow Me." To Nathanael He said, "Before Philip found you I saw you." To Nicodemus He said, You must be "born from above." With that last illustration we pause a moment to remark that it is at least arresting that He is never recorded as having said that to anyone else. It is true that He so said it as to show that it applies to every human being; but it is equally arresting that He is not reported as having said it to anyone else personally. He was employing the method necessary in the case of the man and this He ever did.[117]

In recounting the stories of people who had an encounter with Jesus, Morgan points out that Jesus offered living water to the Samaritan woman who came to the well to draw water and he offered fellowship to Zaccheus who was despised by many.[118] Jesus' adaptation of the presentation of the message of salvation to the spiritual condition and social context of each individual should motivate Bible storyers to take the socio-religious context of individuals and people groups into account while preparing the presentation of the stories.

Tom Steffen points out that there is a sense in which Paul did this as he shared the gospel message. He states:

> A comparison of the evangelistic messages used with Jewish and Greek audiences in Acts shows that Paul adapted his message to his audience. When Paul addressed Gentiles he contextualized the message, emphasizing a creation-centered theology, judgment, and Lordship. Jewish audiences heard more about their historical ties with the Old Testament and the promised Messiah. For Paul the audience determined the type of wrapping paper to be used on each evangelism package. Even though the gift never changed, Paul refused a one-wrapping-for all philosophy (1 Cor. 9:20-22; Gal. 1:8, 9).[119]

No one was more zealous of preserving the integrity of the gospel message than the apostle Paul. To the Galatians he says: *"Even if an angel comes with a different message, let him be anathema"* (Gal. 1:8). When it comes to the manner in which the gospel is communicated, no one was more willing to adapt its presentation than the apostle Paul. He was willing to *"become to the Jews as a Jew."* R. C. H. Lenski explains:

> Paul became not a Jew but "as a Jew" by living according to the Jewish fashion among the Jews and by using their forms of teaching when he sought to convert them. While "Jews" and "those under the law" are identical, "Jews" refers to nationality, and "under the law" refers to religion... The Gentiles were *anomai* because they had no legal code from God to regulate them. Paul accommodated himself to

> them by living as if he, too, were without the law. He mingled freely with them and disregarded all Jewish observances which he had followed at other times; he also, as for instance at Athens, formulated his teaching so that it might make the strongest appeal to the Gentile mind. Paul did not, of course, live in a lawless and in a godless fashion when he was among the Gentiles. He was and remained a Christian among the Gentiles even as he was and remained a Christian among the Jews.[120]

Motivated by his desire to reach as many people with the gospel as possible, (1 Cor. 9: 19, 20, 21, 22) Paul was willing to adapt the presentation of the message to the level of understanding of each individual and people group. *Following Paul's example, effective Bible storyers need to be willing to prepare and present the stories in such a way that people in their ministry focus group are able to hear, understand, apply, and retell these stories.*

Adaptability Regarding the Number of Stories

Adaptability on the part of Bible storyers is needed with regard to the number of stories that should be told before getting to the stories that relate more directly to the salvation of the hearers. While knowing the Bible stories are of utmost importance, it must not be assumed that un-reached people groups need to hear and master a specific number of stories before they can come to a saving knowledge of Christ. Steffen observes that in light of the fact that "the New Testament alludes to over 100 Old Testament events, some difficult choices must be made to keep the content load manageable."[121] He provides helpful insights when he critiques McIlwain's argument that the example of the Apostles needs to be followed in providing an Old Testament foundation for the presentation of the gospel message. He states:

> McIlwain (1987) argues that the apostles began their evangelism by using the Old Testament to emphasize God's dealings with

such historical people as Abraham, Moses, David and then linked them to Christ as revealed in Jesus (Acts 2:22-36; 3:13-26; 10:34-43; 13:16-41; 17:2,3). All of these passages cited, however, deal with Jewish audiences predominantly, except Acts 10 which is the account of the god-fearer Cornelius who no doubt knew the Old Testament well. Conspicuously absent in the preceding list are the two passages that deal specifically with Gentiles – Acts 14:8-20 and 17:16-34.[122]

The purpose in telling the Old Testament stories is not to tell about the characters *per se*, but about God's dealings with mankind. When people ask why they are accountable to the Christian God, the Creation stories, as well as many of the judgment stories, serve to tell why. When people have an erroneous concept of sin, the stories help to define the matter of disobedience, wickedness, and depravity of mankind and the resulting consequences. It is music to the storyer's ears when the people say after hearing one of the Old Testament stories: "We are like those people. God will surely punish us!" The Old Testament stories help a people to see their sinfulness before a righteous God and that they cannot save themselves from His wrath—cannot provide their own salvation. If people do not understand they are sinners, then what value is a Savior? The term "tipping point" applies here—listeners need to hear enough stories so they reach their own tipping point of understanding their sinfulness and thirsting for the salvation God has promised to provide.

The initial concept of CBS called for beginning with Creation in Genesis and continuing through Old Testament stories to at last come to the story of Jesus. Among those who have some existing knowledge of Jesus it is not infrequent for them to ask "When will we get to the story of Jesus?" Among those who do have this knowledge and access and familiarity with the Bible, it may be best to begin with the story of Jesus and then later return to the Old Testament as part of discipling. Situations calling for this approach have been termed "*Jesus First, Genesis Second.*" If people are ready to hear the story of Jesus with the stories and Jesus' teaching leading to faith, then it may be prudent to begin where the people are and take them immediately to Jesus. Christy Brawner in her set of evangelism story lessons uses only seven stories from the Gospel of Matthew.[123]

This variation has been productive in many settings but should be used with care and not assuming that all listeners are ready for the story of Jesus with no real understanding of their accountability to God, a concept of sin that is biblical, and a realization they cannot save themselves from God's judgment. When time with people is very short then the stories of Jesus are primary. In some South Asian situations worship groups have formed resulting from miraculous healing in Jesus' name resulting in a desire for people to know the "Jesus God" and worship him.[124]

Storyers, however, must be aware of the fact that in some settings telling just a few stories may create a problem due to the fact that the listeners are not prepared to make an informed decision when the invitation is given. It can be a demanding task to sandwich a set of Bible story lessons between local religious festivals, agricultural seasons, or even the missionary's own personal schedule. Some missiological strategists, not understanding this restriction, have counseled missionaries to "Tell a few stories, explain the gospel, give an invitation, and plant a church." The "few stories" may not be adequate to prepare listeners for the gospel presentation and invitation. I still remember the people in a Southeast Asian country asking: "Why are we accountable to the Christian God?" Clearly they were not ready for a few stories, some explanation and an invitation. In fact an expanded set of Creation stories along with many stories that tell of man's accountability to God were needed.[125]

A rule of thumb, that has helped many in deciding how many stories to employ, relates to the list of biblical truths that must be taught and most significant worldview issues that need to be emphasized. It will take more time to teach some truths and issues some settings than in others. The storyer perhaps will have to use as many as 5-7 stories to address certain worldview issues and biblical truths.

On an average this worked out around 35-40 stories. Obviously, where there is openness and some prior understanding, the list could be much shorter. Where there is deep spiritual ignorance or resistance or persecution to deal with, the list could be longer as needed. The list of stories can always be edited with experience in use. In actual practice the exact list of stories may differ somewhat from group to group. There have been instances where additional stories were needed. Sometimes this meant having to go back to earlier stories in review and then inserting the new stories that were needed.

The storyer responds to the listeners and their progress in understanding and responding. The story list at times also included affirming stories that were intended to strengthen favorable attitudes to the Bible truths. Also, typically in the longer story sets the ratio of OT to NT stories would average 3/2. As the story list shortened the story selection would shift toward 1/1 and with even shorter story sets the average was 1/2 or 1/3 and if the time was very short, then only the stories of Jesus.[126]

The question regarding the number of stories (Old Testament and New Testament) that need to be shared before presenting the claims of Christ is not an easy one to answer. It cannot be reduced to a simple number or formula. Among other factors, the religious background and the receptivity of the people group to the Gospel message must be taken into account. *While these analyses are done, however, there must be a disciplined sense of urgency that is guided by sensitivity to the Holy Spirit so that people will be given an opportunity to receive Christ and to worship him in congregations of believers as soon as they understand the Gospel message and are willing to make a commitment to follow him the rest of their lives.*

Adaptability Regarding Story Sets

While it is often necessary to acquaint Bible storying trainees with existing story sets, utilizing these without making any adaptations to the local cultural group will lessen the impact that the storying process can make. Jeremy Taliaferro explains:

> One weakness we have seen is using Storying tracts that were created for another people group. This is a quick fix that carries serious problems in the long run. We teach our teams how to custom-make a story set for a specific people group. We spend a lot of time on this because we feel it pays off in the long run. We custom make a story set for each people group, we do not start with a core group of stories. We do not want to get in a rut or be lazy with our preparation. This customizing of the story sets has really helped us to see the people latch on to the stories because they relate to the stories on a deeper level.[127]

Donald Barger voices a similar concern when he says:

> Another weakness has been an attempt at using generic sets with people who don't really understand the entire process of how to do storying. I have seen that this strategy starts out well but doesn't finish well because people become discouraged and begin to mix oral strategies with other methods which often undermine the orality emphasis. I believe that our responsibility is to coach storiers through the process over a long period of time.[128]

As Taliaferro and Barger explain, it takes much more work to customize a story set than to merely use an existing one. Customizing obviously requires doing the work it takes to understand a people group's worldview (including bridges, barriers, and gaps) as well as other cultural characteristics that need to be taken into account in selecting, crafting, and telling the stories. While it takes more work, the results are much greater because the people group will understand and identify with the stories much more readily than if they hear story sets prepared for groups in other cultures.

Adaptability Regarding Meeting Place

Adaptability is needed regarding the place in which Bible stories are shared. Thora Broyles gives an example of this when she states:

> The program is time intensive and yet we have structured it in a way that it can operate without facilities other than a place to meet. This could be a tree. But rain causes problems with that. Last Sunday afternoon we were chased out of the open sided *patam* by rain and wind and had to return to the church building where noise was a terrible problem. [129]

The point that has been made regarding house churches applies to Bible storying. Meeting in whatever space is available in the community can facility the reproducibility of the congregations that are started. Caution, however, needs to be exercised to ensure that no negative or conflicting messages are sent with regards to the place in which people meet. In one village, for example, a member of a people group told the missionary: "It would be wonderful if the stories you told were really true." The missionary assured this person that they were true. To which the person replied: "Well, in our village when our leaders want to tell a true story they stand under that tree."[130]

Adaptability Regarding Methodology

Steve Flook, who has made a significant contribution to Bible Storying work in the Dominican Republic, believes that inflexibility in methodology can lead to the lack of productivity in church planting. He explains:

> Weaknesses in training are caused when we try to program the CBS strategy as if it were a cookie cutter. We have to remember that we are working with people with all different kinds of backgrounds and personalities and the training that is presented must be curtailed to each person's personality. For example: One person we were working with was an owner of

a small business; therefore he did not require much training in the area of responsibility as did another person who had difficulties holding down a job. Also from our experience the people who were teachable and dependable were people who had a job or owned a small business because they understood responsibility and they had dreams and goals and were able to grasp the big vision of reaching their own people for Christ.[131]

Part of adapting the methodology to the socio-cultural backgrounds of the people involves the utilization of an appropriate form of sharing the Bible stories. Undoubtedly the chronological method of sharing Bible stories is the best know and most widely used. Today, however, many methods of Bible storying are being used. These methods include situational Bible storying, life-story encounters, and many other means described in our segment on "Additional Resources" (appendix L)

Church Starting Strategies

A second factor in developing strategies for using Bible Storying in church planting relates to using the proper and adapted strategies for church starting. In Chapter one, we reviewed the manner in which Paul progressed quite naturally from communicating the gospel to gathering the believers into congregations. This did not, however, happen automatically. Paul employed serious internationality in developing his strategies. Contemporary Bible storyers need to have the same type of intentionality if their efforts are going to result in the establishment of churches. Among the elements in the process that will contribute to church starting are having a biblical definition of church, a willingness to do fast tracking, knowing when to draw the net, creating a sense of community, incorporating converts into the body of believers, transitioning from a storying group to a church, and leading the group to become an autonomous church.

Biblical Definition of Church

A church that formed as a result of a radio program in Bangalore, India, set an example of what constitutes a church. In that city several older churches existed, having well-paid pastors with theological education, and possessing their own buildings. But in a slum area when people heard the radio programs in their language they were convicted of sin and wanted to profess their faith in Christ. They did not know what to do. So the group sent a delegation to the local mission office to ask what they should do.

The staff evangelist led the group to profess their faith and 12 were baptized. Immediately the group began meeting in the home of a shoe cobbler to listen to the daily broadcasts and worship. The man in whose home they met did not have a clue what to do or how to preach. Their devotionals were often children quoting Bible verses they learned. The group quickly took on body life and when I would visit their services to speak they would lead me from home to home to pray for community members.

When the church outgrew that house the landlord insisted they move to a larger house. The man who was their leader was, I suspect, non-literate. That group, however, had taken on the characteristics of a New Testament church (in evangelism, discipleship, ministry, worship, fellowship, prayer, and reproduction, (Acts 2:40-47) even though they could not meet the local convention's qualifications to be recognized as such. Many small groups have come out of the storying sessions by storying evangelists and have begun functioning with a body life that characterizes them as true churches.[132]

It is important to encourage the new emerging groups of believers to work cooperatively with existing ecclesiastical organizations. At times, however, it becomes necessary to encourage ecclesiastical organizations to refrain from imposing extra-biblical standards upon new congregations in order to officially recognize them as churches. Some of these extra-biblical standards at times include:[133]

- Requiring church buildings;

- Making literacy a requirement for church leadership;

- Ordaining only those who have received formal theological education;

- Requiring a specified number of members to establish a church;

- Recognizing only full-time professional church leaders;

- Insisting on only one church planting model.

There is a sense in which some of the standards mentioned here can actually be a blessing if the means and resources are available to attain them. There is also a sense, however, in which the imposition of extra-biblical requirements can stifle, if not kill, an emerging congregation. A biblical definition of church, therefore, is needed in order to impact entire regions of the world with the gospel message.

The Baptist Faith and Message of the Southern Baptist Convention gives the following definition of a church:

> A New Testament church of the Lord Jesus Christ is an autonomous local congregation of baptized believers, associated by covenant in the faith and fellowship of the gospel; observing the two ordinances of Christ, governed by His laws, exercising the gifts, rights, and privileges invested in them by His Word; and seeking to extend the gospel to the ends of the earth."[134]

In his discussion on the classic marks of a true church, Stan Norman asserts:

> A true church is united in fellowship and the bonds of the Holy Spirit with a congregation set apart from the world in pursuit of holiness in worship and service. A true church is the unity of all the redeemed of all the ages as will ultimately be revealed and enjoyed in the final state. A true church is committed and submitted absolutely to the revelation of Jesus Christ as given by the apostles. A true church

manifests its authenticity in the right preaching of the Word, the right administration of the ordinances, and the right administration of church discipline.[135]

It is important to note that neither this definition of a church nor the classic marks of a church include the extra-biblical requirements we discussed above. Larry Kreider echoes this thought when he states:

> The New Testament *church* was defined as the *people*. Believers did not *go* to church or *join* the church; they *were* the church. All members functioned as priests because everyone served as ministers. Each person got on-the-job training and learned how to make disciples. These followers of Jesus practiced their faith in spiritual families, met in homes and radically changed the world. They grew in number as they obeyed God's Word and shared resources and spiritual blessings. They multiplied into more and more groups of believers meeting in homes, all networking together. They were the original house church networks![136]

A truly biblical definition of a church is foundational for the establishment of untold numbers of churches through the utilization of Bible Storying strategies.

Adequate Timing

A very important factor related to Bible Storying and church planting is that of the timing that is employed. Another way of stating this is that in some settings there does not appear to be a very clear understanding about the type of decision that people need to make to identify fully as followers of Jesus Christ. This relates to the gradualness of the process of storying in some settings as well as the pace at which the stories are told.

The gradualness of the process

Unless the storyer is aware of it, the storying process can be so gradual that it does not lead to a clear-cut decision to receive Christ and to identify with a group of fellow believers.

LaNette Thompson explains:

> It is so subtle that new believers don't know what happened to them. When family asks why they want to leave their religion to embrace a new one, they do not know how to respond. They may say, "It's the truth," but they cannot go beyond that. The beauty of CBS is that it breaks down the worldview barriers with truths from Scripture, but this breakdown happens gradually over a long period of time. Unfortunately, new believers often cannot explain "in a nutshell" what they believe to others. [137]

In one sense, however, this strength of Bible Storying can become a weakness. In its commendable effort to employ a win/win strategy so that the lines of communication will remain open and the person will have an opportunity to hear the gospel story, there may be a subtle danger of not leading people to a definite point of decision to receive Christ as their only Savior and of identifying with his followers. While it must be acknowledged that this process needs to be done differently in the different cultural settings and that the cultural form which a church takes will be different among the different people groups, conscious decisions must be made on the part of the new believers if, from a biblical perspective, they are to become genuine disciples of Jesus Christ. Failure to bring people to decision will undermine witnessing as well as church planting efforts among that people group.

Once, when CBS was in its early developmental stage, a storyer from the Philippines was sharing the concept of CBS in Indonesia and told of using a set of 54 (27 OT stories & 27 NT) Bible stories in his teaching. Along about story number 32 one of the women listeners, who apparently was coming under conviction sooner than the others, expressed that she wanted to believe on Jesus. This caught the storyer off-guard who told her that she must wait because he had not finished all the stories.

Because in areas where there is some existing knowledge of the gospel this early response does happen rather frequently, those of us who train Bible Storyers recommend taking the early responders aside and testing their understanding, providing a basic summary gospel presentation and give an invitation. Then the listener is told to be patient as the others do not yet understand as they do. In reality, it is not always possible to take a listener aside privately as inevitably others will want to listen. The point is to address that early responder as needed while continuing to lead the group to that same readiness.[138]

On the other hand, many persons living in oral cultures may need the time to make important decisions. They want to think about it. It takes reaching a *tipping point* at which the heart responds to the Holy Spirit's urging and so that a decision is made favorable to change belief and finally to accept and act upon the biblical truth leading to salvation. In this case it is leaving the old way and following Jesus. In Bali, and also reported among the Aukan people of Suriname, part of the evangelism and church planting process involved dealing with a people's fear of change—fear of reprisal by evil spirits.

Also fear of persecution is a deterrent to change until a person is assured that following Jesus is better than fearing man. So rushing to a decision-making time does not deal adequately with fears that hinder professing faith in Christ or forming a New Testament church. As experience with a people dictates, the storyer must alter the story set either to shorten it to maintain urgency or lengthen it as needed to reach the faith tipping point.[139]

The pace that is employed

The pace at which the storying process takes occurs also has a bearing on the church planting that takes place. LaNette Thompson observes:

> We have become content to go slowly. We have too often gone ahead with our schedule

(a story a week) rather than be sensitive to the spiritual needs of the people. The truth is that if the Spirit is moving and people are being convicted and we are not yet to the end of the Evangelism Track, we need to take them there as quickly as possible. We can always return and do the last stories in more depth. We want people to be interested in what will happen next. If they are only interested, we should continue as usual. However, if they are CONVICTED, if the Holy Spirit is speaking to someone or several in a group, we should not make them wait. It is appropriate to fast-track from the beginning or to do an even shorter presentation such as the TRT - Training for Rural Trainers - for people who are open.[140]

Dr. Grant Lovejoy also expresses concerns about the pace at which CBS takes place in some settings and the possible connection between this and the lack of productivity in church starting in some settings. He states:

Leading CPM advocates have suggested that the very pace of traditional CBS does not adequately convey urgency. People who have spent months slowly and gradually coming to awareness and acceptance of the gospel message do not know how to move with urgency to share it with others. I'm wondering if there is truth to this.[141]

Steven King voices a similar concern when he states:

I have seen one team in the past develop a long evangelism track which they could not complete before their audience turned over. They were never able to start a church because they were losing their audience. My observation is that their story track included much more than what is necessary to win a person to Christ, even within the cultural context. Adaptations that reduce the evangelism track to the essentials of the gospel along with the essential stories to deal with significant barriers to the gospel are more successful.[142]

Here again, in our CBS training we often emphasize the option of fast tracking with those who are ready to receive Christ and to identify with a group of believers locally. It is obvious that there are instances where this is not being done and there may be more of a commitment to "follow the plan" than to be sensitive to what the Holy Spirit is doing in the lives of the people.

Working with a rural group in Thailand, a missionary was told to slow down. The people said that he was making their "head hurt." So there is the urgency of the gospel and the need to evangelize others, but there is the oral culture characteristic that one cannot be rushed into making decisions. Part of this is a cultural characteristic. The previously referred to "tipping point" is reached after the new spiritual information reaches an urgency level requiring response by the listener. Among tribals being trained in CBS in Orissa, there was a sense of urgency by those hearing the stories to tell the stories to others. In his *Stories From Storytellers*[143] Paul F. Koehler reports many instances in India where those hearing the Bible stories immediately have an urgency to believe on Jesus, receive baptism, and to tell others. In a predominantly Hindu culture this is a bold move.[144]

Fast-tracking

The timing of storying is often altered by the need for fast-tracking. Fast-tracking simply means that the storying process is accelerated. After being involved in CBS for a time I found out that one of the strongest reasons for fast-track storying was that of probing for potential response. By using a fast-paced story set that involved the stories of families and peoples in the OT stories, and then the compassionate stories of Jesus up through the Passion story, the people were emotionally moved. Then my team asked if they would like for one of us to return and tell more of these stories. We used a similar "tell and ask for permission to return" approach in the hospital ward storying in Tanjungkarang, Sumatra, Indonesia, and in the home visitation for prayer ministry in several other South Asian countries.

The other reason for fast-tracking was that of impact discipling with the panorama of the Redemption Story and several places where the people saw the danger or God's displeasure with lack of obedience—Lot leaving Canaan where God had promised to bless, the 12 spies story, the people's falling away in Judges after promising to be faithful, Saul's disobedience, Solomon's folly, the idolatry and stubbornness of the people in the kingdoms, and finally the hostility against Jesus and rejection by his own people. This as a whole seemed to spur them to go tell others among their people.

In the Khond Hills among the Kui the hot season was the evangelism season as it was too dry to farm and so the men were free to travel. Later when the men were taught the bamboo planting technique, they would tell the Bible stories as they worked with local people planting bamboo as a cash crop. At one time new churches were coming every five days on average according to former missionary Calvin Fox. I believe that in many situations that churches were planted sooner where the missionaries lived among a people or had daily contact with them rather than commuting on some basis.[145]

The Creation to Christ (C2C) fast-tracks are becoming more popular, both for probing for response, and as an introduction to a more traditional gospel presentation. The shorter story sets are often easier for oral learners to remember and retell. Storyers seek to reach a balance between being thorough to reach the conviction tipping point and dealing with elements of syncretism, and that of urgency that LaNette mentioned, and accelerating CPM if possible without drawing it out over a long period. One compromise is to go for the accelerated gospel story presentation and then have an extended discipleship. Some have found this approach works by beginning with the stories of Jesus and then later in discipling going back to Genesis and the OT stories and a review of the Gospels to strengthen new believers. There is not one ideal strategy for all people groups. Again, this points out the need for a good understanding of the listener worldview and some experience in seeing how fast or brief you can go without undue compromise in understanding and faith.

The explosion of churches and worship groups among the Bhojpuri in India happened with mostly non-literate worship leaders and pastors. In a place like that I would have gone to the stories of Jesus and his peace rather than a long strategy of OT stories, then the Gospel stories stretching over a long period of time. In this Indian setting the group reached a Samaritan experience like Jesus referred to—no need to wait four months for the harvest, the fields were already white. There the problem was not that there was a lack of workers in the harvest, but a lack of trained workers who could rightly divide the word of faith.

While it is true that there are numerous situations where fast-tracking becomes necessary due to extenuating circumstances, storyers should be careful not to be in such a hurry to get to the Gospel that they hamper the group's ability to understand the message of the Bible. Taliaferro sounds this word of caution when he states:

> Another problem we have seen is extremely short story sets. We agree that there is an urgency to get to the story of Christ ASAP. But we also have to come to realize that the Old Testament is also the story of Christ. I believe this problem stems from other traditional forms that are dictating when and where storying should take place. If you tell 1 story a week on Sundays in a church building it will take you 10 months to finish a 40 story set. If you plan on telling stories in homes every other day it will take two and a half months. If you are storying every day it will take less than 6 weeks. I feel like when we think of storying as something that can happen anywhere and anytime it will allow us to have our cake and eat it too. We can have longer story sets and still get to the story of Christ with urgency.[146]

Drawing the Net

Another factor that contributes to church planting is having a clear understanding of when and how to draw the net, that is, call for decision. In East Asia some listeners came under conviction from the OT stories and then rejoiced at the Good News in the Gospel and Acts stories. There was no need for convincing them outside of the stories and lessons. Others understood the essentials but needed some time to think about what to do while some were urging them to act on it. Many times if we could teach the leaders sufficiently then the people would follow when the leaders responded. We realize that for some workers this type of response raises questions about whether the people truly had crisis conversions or not. Such responses are realities in communal societies.

Many of the younger missionaries had not lived among a people long enough to understand the culture of conversion from the faith of their fathers to a new faith. In my experience I saw everything from hungry hearts that just latched onto spiritual truth and by the time you reached the Resurrection they were ready to know what to do. Others were more Asian in being philosophical in their approach to Christianity. After much time and much teaching during which they became closer and closer until at some random moment they considered themselves Christians. Some of the tribal people in Thailand used a number system to let you know where they were in their response. I remember one man in Bob Stewart's area who told us he was at ten but he said that soon he hoped to be at two or even one. At that point he would be at acceptance. Some were just practical and wanted to see what worked best![147]

An understanding of the spiritual condition as well as cultural customs can help the Bible storyer, after much prayer, to know when to draw the net.

Sense of Community

Charles Madinger and his colleagues stress the importance of a sense of community in the utilization of oral strategies. He states:

> Orality works when the message is relationally received. That relationships stem from hearing the same dialect (not just language), from known voices (not just actors), with village informational gate-keepers (not just anybody)

in a familiar community (insiders, not outsiders).[148]

People who are being reached through Bible Storying methodologies need to have a sense of community if they are to become a part of Christian congregations. Jim Slack expressed this when he was interviewed by Grant Lovejoy.

> Slack thinks that building a sense of community is crucial. This depends on the presence of the storyer and the respect that listeners have for the storyer. The community should be taught that they (not individuals) are the keepers of the story. The community is responsible for preserving, perpetuating, and proclaiming these stories.[149]

While often there is a discussion about the number of Old Testament stories that need to be told in order to get to "the gospel," we may need to look at two alternatives related to the matter of instilling a sense of community in the new believers. First, there are numerous instances in which the people of God gathered to worship him and to fellowship with one another. The stories related to the Tabernacle emphasize the importance of corporate worship. The church planting storyer could well be planting the seeds for the formation of congregations even as Old Testament stories are being told. Second, it could be that a New Testament story (such as the coming together of the congregation in Corinth) could be shared (as a preview) even as the Old Testament series of stories is being shared.

H. R. Weber places a strong emphasis on community life as a catalyst for internalizing God's Word on the part of oral learners. He believes that group dynamics are ever present in 'primitive' communities, and their consideration leads to the following conclusions for the missionary encounter with oral learners:

- We must not address the individual as an individual but as one of his group and one with his group... A converted individual still living in the dynamics of an unconverted group, and under the power of an unconverted group spirit, will almost certainly renounce his Christian faith.

- The best missionary approach to illiterates living in 'primitive' communities is the witness to Christ by the *koinonia*, by Christian group living... A Christian 'cell' should demonstrate the dynamic Gospel, patiently and hopefully, before any relevant word can be spoken.

- The evangelizing *koinonia* can only come into being when lay people have a full share in the life of the 'fellowship of the Holy Ghost', as in the church in Corinth where, according to 1 Cor. 14.26, every individual contributed something to the building up of the fellowship. This sharing, this participation is therefore the most important element in the communication of the Gospel to illiterates.

- Group dynamics are only Christian group dynamics as long as the wind of the spirit is felt.[150]

Incorporation

An additional challenge to the task of starting churches in connection with Bible Storying methodologies is that of incorporating new believers into a group that begins to take on the characteristics of a church. This has several dimensions. One challenge is the incorporation of individuals. The other is the incorporation of groups.

Incorporation of individuals

It is obvious that individuals need to be incorporated into the local body of Christ in order for a local church to be established. This, however, is not an easy task in situations where there is a general resistance to the gospel on the part of the local society. Some in the past have counseled strongly against attempting to plant a church among those who are unsaved. For this reason they have advised a time of reviewing the evangelism stories first to strengthen new believers who responded to the initial evangelism track and invitation, to provide the missing key stories to those who joined the storying sessions later and missed all or most of the OT background to the Gospel, and finally to provide an extended invitation to slow responders who, either needed more time in making their decision, or who had still unanswered questions or fears about "changing religions."

We have a similar concern because we do not want to bring over and include unsaved listeners for planting the church as the stories and lessons are now primarily going to be addressing how believers formed into communities of faith for worship, ministry, and evangelism. But in communal societies it is very difficult to exclude non-believers from a meeting or service. So it is extremely important to be thorough in evangelism and any needed review of evangelism to be sure that the majority, if not all of the listeners, has made decisions for Christ. Now this is difficult in many places because out of fear some will not openly acknowledge a profession of faith. Some will do this, after either waiting to see what happens to others who do go public or someone in their family asks them why they are different and so the decision comes out, or the Spirit simply prompts them to do so and quells any fears they may have.

The challenge of incorporating new believers into an emerging church group is made even more difficult when the setting is one in which there is resistance to the gospel message. The answer, however, is not to postpone the starting of a church indefinitely. New believers need to come together to participate in worship, prayer, fellowship, ministry, baptism, and the Lord's Supper so that their faith might be strengthened and their witness might be stronger in their community. The answer may be found in having two tracks going on simultaneously as long as it is necessary. In the Evangelism Track the stories that lead people to salvation will need to continue to be told as long as there are unbelievers in the group. The other track can be a combination of Discipleship and Church Starting. This track will need to be only for believers who are ready to be discipled and to start gathering in meetings that enable them to begin to function as an emerging church.

Incorporation will need to be done in ways that take the characteristics of the local culture into account. It must be kept in mind, however, that if there is no incorporation, churches will not be formed. In Acts 2:41 we find that those who believed were baptized and added to the local body of believers.

Incorporation of groups

On the mission field, interaction with the literate established conventions and their leaders can be a challenge. The oral leaders did not fit in with their urban literate counterparts. I was handicapped by my inability to be with all these groups more often to encourage them and continue teaching them. Because of their low literacy and limited education they could not easily be taught via printed materials though those with some literacy cherished any printed lesson or teaching they could get.[151] Finding ways for people at the various literacy levels to fellowship with one another can create a spirit of unity and harmony. When it comes to evangelizing and discipling having compatible groups may be more productive. Having trained leaders who aggressively gather believers is crucial.

Transitioning to church

One of the most crucial factors in effective church planting is implementing a plan to transition from a storying group to a church. It is important to begin planting the seeds for church status from the very beginning of the Bible storying process. This can be accompanied by teaching worship songs along the way and gradually introducing simple prayer for God to help understand his Word, to later intercessory prayer and praise and thanksgiving prayer.

Some have strongly cautioned about having worship or doing "church" things while teaching as the people were not yet believers and had not yet a reason to worship. Many of our newer missionaries do begin modeling worship earlier along the way. Singing is very attractive among many Asian and African peoples. In so many cultures there are listeners who are believers (or God-fearers, or Jesus-followers, even if not yet believers), who are singers and want to put the stories into their song forms and there are people who are worship-oriented like many of the Hindus who quickly want to adore or worship those they respect.

Stories are often put into song along the way or other worship-type songs are introduced and learned by the listeners. Some of the OT worship stories are helpful for this. When Bible storyers get to the church planting stories in Acts, they need to demonstrate and include worship activities more clearly and intentionally in addition to the teaching from the stories. Many of our missionaries did begin adding in pre-worship activities as the stories progress and get nearer the end. Bible storyers also need to be adaptable and respond to each people group rather than be locked into a rigid model.[152]

A Hindu background believer pastor told me that Christianity takes away their festivals that are important to Indian people. Some Christian groups are emphasizing a recovery of celebrating the OT festivals that is apparently attractive to the people. Through these experiences, I found that festival stories were liked by the listeners. Gathering people for worship should be planned from the very beginning of the storying process and not an afterthought.

Church Autonomy

Autonomy also appears to be a factor that contributes to the establishment of churches in connection with Bible Storying methodologies. As Lovejoy points out, emerging congregations often experience pressure on the part of established work to conform to their standards and method-ologies. He explains:

> Pressure to conform coming from surrounding churches, denominations, and the like is found in many places, regardless of whether one uses storying or another method of evangel-ism and church planting. We must prize the example of the church at Antioch over the church at Jerusalem. (Antioch sent laymen to the Jerusalem conference, where they won the argument with Peter and the other Jerusalem leaders. They went back to Antioch with their autonomy secured.)[153]

As much as possible an effort should be made to prevent the churches that are established as a result of Bible Storying strategies from being pressed into a mold that stifles their growth and reproduction. In order for this to be avoided the leaders of established churches need to be oriented with regard to orality and Bible Storying methodologies. Also, the leaders in the new congregations need to be equipped to exercise leadership in their settings. Lovejoy elaborates:

> Though Slack and coworkers did want good relationships with the local groups, they were quick to put responsibility for those new groups into the hands of the new believers. They taught them to lead, expected them to lead, and got far enough out of the picture that the local people had to lead if anything was going to happen.[154]

There is a sense in which it is easier to start churches through the use of Bible Storying strategies in areas where there are no churches and there is not already a church tradition in place. Unfortunately that often is not the case even in isolated areas in a given country. Often the leaders in the capital city, who very likely are literate, attempt to set the standard even for people in isolated areas. This, therefore, requires the dual task alluded to above: Leaders of established churches need to be oriented with regard to orality and Bible Storying methodologies. The leaders in the new congregations of oral communicators need to be equipped to exercise leadership in their settings.

Training Strategies

If Bible storying efforts are to result in the establishment of churches, local leaders must be trained. In this segment we describe the lack of trained leaders as well as strategies to train leaders in their various stages of literacy.

A lack of leaders can significantly delay starting churches. I have had groups from radio programs wanting to form but denied a church because there was no leader. In the teaching I was doing with the Bengalis and later the Kuis, I saw that if there were strong leaders who were competent to preach and teach, when the nascent church was forming, they could take it to coalesce into a New Testament church. I enjoyed several years of five-day training sessions but later the decision was made in Bangladesh to cut this down to three and later to just one day to reduce budget costs for transportation, lodging, and food. Also many of the men were daily wage earners and their families went without food when the men were not working. So, longer training periods worked a serious hardship on them and their families. One day or even three days was not enough for a new person though it could help those who already had the longer training.[155] Finding appropriate times to train local leaders is indeed a challenge. Without adequate training, however, it is extremely difficult to have on-going church planting efforts.

Also training is not a one-time event but must be an ongoing process for oral learners. The training must be a balance between knowledge, how to use (practicum) and actual use (experience) for oral leaders. It was also very important to hear the difficulties each trainee faced and as much as possible to anticipate these and train accordingly. One storyer I had worked with in India told me one day that "I had no face." He went on to explain that when I failed I did not become discouraged or ashamed to try again. He said that it was difficult for him to do that. In time he did grow in boldness and "lost his face, too!"

In other circumstances the problem was with literates in the training sessions. These literates needed to understand that they must learn the appropriate ways to teach their own people who may not have the same literacy competency. In so many of these places, the majority of believers were women who definitely were neither literate nor educated even if barely literate.[156]

Steven King expresses a similar concern for the need to train leaders to ensure that storying methodologies will result in church planting. He explains:

> I have seen CBS training done over a three or four day period. I don't think you do more than familiarize people with the process in this short a time. To leave it there usually means that the team will not carry it through to a good implementation. The Xtreme Team trains CBS over a three month period. Thus far this is the only effective training I have seen.[157]

Keith Stamps suggests that a period of mentoring could be very helpful for those being introduced to CBS for the first time. He explains:

> This brings up an issue I see in our traditional training approaches: the need for mentoring and follow up once the person is actually going through the process in the field.[158]

In addition to not taking sufficient time to train the leaders there is the issue of the methodology that is used to train them. A possible inappropriate use is that of working from a notebook or set of printed lessons before the people rather than working with good preparation or memory and perhaps just a Bible in hand if appropriate.

I had to work through interpreters as I did not speak any of the languages where I worked. So my interpreters became my first trainees. In addition we worked as a team which was good for them as they went with me and saw what I did. I also asked for and followed their advice, or we discussed it if there was a difference.[159]

An additional challenge in training leaders beyond the instruction they receive through CBS methodologies is the training that is done in the local theological institutions. Keith Stamps alludes to this concern when he states:

> Related to this has been the difficulty of convincing established theological educators in our various countries and helping them to realize what lost people in their communities, barrios and rural areas are like. Scholars too often see the world as divided between literate and lazy resulting in their ignoring the rich orality around them. How they teach their students will control to a great extent how their students pastor their church, train their people and as a result how the membership will reach and disciple the lost.[160]

Approaches to Training Leaders

One of the most important factors in ensuring that Bible Storying leads to church planting is the training of the storyers. Grant Lovejoy affirms this when he says:

> My hunch is that the solution to the "getting to church" issue lies in a combination of more intentionality, better training and materials that fully equip personnel to make the transition from believers to church, and more follow up to see that it actually happens. [161]

Training leaders for Bible Storying that leads to church planting is at times a three-fold task: Training leaders who are advanced literates; Training leaders who are basic literates; and Training primary oral leaders. [162]

Training leaders who are advanced literates

Training leaders who are advanced literates should focus not only on Bible Storying methodologies but on the learning styles of oral communicators as well. [163] **It is absolutely essential for advanced literates to be aware of the factors that oral communicators hear, understand, retain, and retell to the degree that oral methods of communication are employed.** As has been stated earlier, when literate Bible storyers employ literate means to reach and train oral learners, reproduction is not going to result. For example, working from a notebook or set of printed lessons with an oral group will impede communication. On the other hand, working with good preparation or memory and perhaps just a Bible in hand is appropriate. This is helpful because oral people will be able to understand and retain the Bible stories more easily and will be able to reproduce the process more readily.

Training leaders who are basic literates

In some situations one might easily get the impression that everyone is an advanced or basic literate. **When it comes to learning, however, it may become evident that many advanced literates or basic literates actually learn better through the use of oral methodologies.**

Thora Broyles found that out when she and her husband, David, were training people through storying methodologies in the United States. She explains:

> There is a new development here in the States. We are being delayed in our return to the field and are seeing some interesting things develop here. This past May I trained a summer missionary to use stories to lead people to the Lord and to disciple them. I was recently told that this young man saw some really good fruit from using this and that the new Christians were growing well in the Lord. We are also having some of the local pastors and others not so local asking us to train them in storying use because many of the newer people coming into the churches do not understand the standard form of sermons or teaching as it is being used here in the states. They are more oral in the way they process information and need a more oral approach. When David or I illustrate by teaching or preaching with a Bible story the pastors say that they saw the lights come on in the eyes of these newer believers for the first time. So it appears that we need to do a lot more teaching here in the states as well so that others here can see good results.[164]

Though we have made this point elsewhere it bears repeating here that **Bible Storying can be effective among all types of oral learners**. This may include those who consider themselves advanced literates or basic literates but whose primary way of learning and communicating is oral. Wayne Dye affirms that many people in the United States may be categorized as "literates" yet, they willingly utilize oral methods of communication. He explains:

> Statistically, a preference for oral communication has been demonstrated repeatedly. In the particular terminology of the Department of Education, about half of all Americans are "semi-literate" meaning that they can read but

seldom do, using only oral and direct visual communication when they have a choice. Clearly, for vast numbers of Americans "literate" meaning knows how to read differs from "literate" meaning prefers written over oral communication.

The movie industry has long recognized the value of stories to bring value change. They have been using these methods and little more to teach their moral values for several generations, and many of us are decrying the resultant changes in American morals... In short, educated people, not just oral communicators, are taught and (over time) changed through well-told stories.

At this point it is worth pondering how Jesus used stories. They were his primary way to teach, not only with First Century Jewish peasants but also when speaking to Pharisees and rulers, all well educated men. This certainly speaks for a storying method of teaching, but also casts doubts on the idea the storying is somehow a method for oral people rather than highly literate. For Jesus, it was the principal way to teach everyone.[165]

Training leaders who are primary oral learners

Training primary oral learners requires that attention be paid not only to the content but also to the thinking processes they employ. According to Ed Beach this requires a concerted effort on the part of the storyer/trainer to understand the way in which oral communicators in their particular people group think and feel. He explains:

> Based on my research and experience (mostly with Mayans, but with others as well), the issue runs way deeper than simply format, and focusing so much on format can actually wind up being somewhat deceptive. The worldview, relational values and expectations, communication expectations and thinking processes

that oral culture people have are vastly different that western literate people. Therein lays the key. Stories are merely a surface manifestation of all that. Stories are like a sky-scraper we see, and the worldview like the foundation and internal structure that is not readily obvious. So, a North American trying to be "oral" will put together a story in one way, and a non-western oral culture person will put together a story about the same thing in a very different way. Merely delivering the news/facts/fable/whatever in story format does not automatically make it rightly under-stood or persuasive. The point is that we need to learn to understand how orals think inside their heads and hearts. [166]

From the very beginning the story trainer who comes from outside the culture of the people group needs to be aware that the insider has a better understanding of the local culture than any outsider. Paul F. Koehler points this out when he states:

In my experience, when indigenous storytell-ers begin telling the Bible stories to others, they quickly grasp the cultural dynamics by noting the responses, questions and reactions of the listeners to the stories they tell. As a re-sult, often they choose to tell different stories than the ones I would have selected... For example, the Creation story in Genesis chapter one has consistently been one of the most popular stories in a wide variety of cultures where my trainees are working. Another is the story of Sodom and Gomorrah. If the story trainer does a good job of teaching the story-tellers a broad range of Bible stories, their ability to apply the stories in their own context will supersede anything an outsider might devise... Instead of spending large amounts of time up front attempting to exegete the culture, I have found the best way for us is to teach insiders to tell the stories (and motivate them to do so). As their oral canon develops it will tend to emphasize stories that are most appropriate to the cultural worldview of that people.[167]

Koehler's anthropological training and experience with people groups have taught him that the learning preferences of oral learners must be taken into account in any efforts geared at equipping them for effective Bible storying. He states:

> What we are talking about here is the development of a core model for beginners. I am suggesting that for the "non-specialist" who simply wants to get started using biblical storytelling, a detailed, intensive, upfront world view study is probably overkill...

> A fundamental difference in learning preferences between oral and literate people influences this discussion. Literates tend to want to understand everything up front before we actually start doing it. That's how our schooling has taught us to think and so we are comfortable with that. However oral communicators are not capable of learning like this or of retaining such knowledge. In oral cultures, learning is a hands-on activity; oral communicators typically learn by doing a task or by observing someone else do it.

> For them the accumulation of knowledge is integrated with praxis... What I would say to a storyteller trainer who is working with oral people is, "Let's just start doing it and learn together as we go." For the oral learner knowledge is cyclical. They like to start with a "simple" whole. Then the bells and whistles can be added little by little. We can do it their way.[168]

In light of the fact that oral communicators learn by observing someone else do it, modeling must be one of the principal approaches that are utilized in training oral leaders. When oral learners are reached for Christ through Bible storying they will not only be in a position to tell the stories to others but to follow the learning pattern they have observed on the part of the Bible storyer. There is a sense in which modeling can lead to mentoring. Fernando and Brenda Larzabal have been doing the type of mentoring that is helping them to see church planting reproduction on their field. They explain:

> We are working with "L" and "J" by mainly asking questions and helping them to think through the issues on a number of areas for their return to the community. One of these areas is the definition of key terms/concepts that they are using. What will the people group church look like? How will the message get to the other four villages? What is their plan to disciple the new believers?
>
> "L" and "J" will return to the community next month and stay until December. They will then come out and stay here in the city for three months so that they can work together with others on the team here in the city to develop more fully their plan and continued strategy and also to get some much needed rest.169

On-going training for oral learners should seek to enable them to continue to learn on their own. Donald Barger considers on-going training essential to effectiveness in church planting when he says: *"Follow-up has been non-existent. We have typically done storying training as an event... a one-time training over a weekend or a week. I am convinced that we need more storying coaching and training."*[170]

Training oral learners should include extensive modeling on the part of the trainers. Taliaferro stresses the importance of doing this when he states:

I would say the most important thing for the training of storyers is constant and varied modeling by experienced storyers. They should see it done over and over by different people in different ways. This takes it beyond theory. They learn stories and are affected by the methodology and therefore are convinced of its relevance.

I would also recommend teaching them to use culturally appropriate objects, gestures, and even sound effects.

We teach them to tell the stories and learn the stories in scenes. They change location for instance when Abraham goes up to the mountain to sacrifice his son. They also learn to alternate body positions during dialogue, how to use their voices, etc.

Let them practice building a story tract. Give them focus on a people group. Let them research, find bridges and barriers. Determine their Purposes for the tract and choose Threads to use throughout the set. Draw up a list of stories and then evaluate which ones are necessary and not based on the Purposes, Bridges, Barriers, and Threads. This is also a good tool for the storyteller in reviewing the entire story and how you want to present it as a whole before you begin telling stories. We have seen this methodology mobilize indigenous believers into action with minimal training. I believe this is the first steps to a CPM. They feel empowered to be missionaries. They feel capable of taking the gospel to their own people and others. They can teach someone else how to do it and see the workers multiply. Thus, the harvests will also multiply.[171]

Donald Barger echoes this when he states:

I believe that orality training has traditionally not modeled what small groups can look like.

Generally speaking, training has been heavily literate and classroom like. This has not always been true but it is common. We have tried to break the training into small groups so that it would model what house church could/should look like. We have the story training create the atmosphere of small group integrating storying, prayer time, worship, and going outside of the class to put it into practice. Takes a bit longer but it pays off because people see the end result that we are after. I would go through a set of stories throughout the week. In place of using power points, use stories that explain the same principles. Have them learn a simple panorama throughout the week and the test would be an oral exam of telling the stories. Have them go out each day and tell stories that they are learning to lost people.[172]

Modeling the Bible storying process can have a very important effect and that is the establishment of a level of trust. In his utilization of oral strategies Charles Madinger has found substantial evidence in the numerous countries where he and his organization have ministered that the source needs to be trusted if the message is to be believed.[173] In training leaders for Bible storying, the more the leaders have an opportunity to come in contact with the storyers the more they will believe their message. Modeling the Bible storying process, therefore, can be a form of incarnating the message.

In addition to modeling Bible storying some, such as Beth Seversen, have found that encouraging people to role-play stories has been very helpful. She explains:

I received a note yesterday saying when the Indians evaluated the conference they thought the Bible Storying was invaluable. I had them role play a story the first day. The second day they had to initiate dialog, lead a pre- story discussion, tell a second story (either a preceding or succeeding story from the

104

evangelism track), lead a post-discussion, end with a verse. It was a wild time as we had to translate into Telegu and Kanada but the Lord was kind and the Indians wholeheartedly participated. Some traveled as much as 18 hours to attend. I do wish we had more time but I left my entire notebook full of stories downloaded from e-mails with two pastors from the two language groups who intend to see the information gets to those who want more.[174]

Another method that has been very helpful in training Bible storyers has been the utilization of songs. In my teaching I noticed that most of the pastors I worked with immediately began teaching their listeners songs. I know that in Africa people have a tendency to remember things better when in song format and sung often. The men that were trained in the Sudan project found that songs attracted the people to hear the stories. So that is one aspect of it. Singing also attracts Hindus in villages. So it may depend on how the songs are used, whether in worship or for teaching. I am a bit more open to permitting singing, especially of praise songs, during the OT stories that are teaching about the characteristics of God. Was it John Wesley who said something about learning our theology from songs?[175]

H.R. Weber affirms the utilization of a wide variety of methods, including songs to communicate effectively with oral learners. He explains:

> A communication that has merely been told cannot be firmly anchored in the mind of the illiterate. He may hear the Bible stories, but in time will forget them or he will transform and confuse them with well-know myths, because he cannot read the Bible, the text of those stories. Moreover, there is this to be said, that illiterates have an amazing ability to learn by heart and to remember. It is advisable, however, to teach illiterates, along with each Bible story, a text which summarizes the story, and a hymn, and in this way to help

them to remember the story. Ways and means must be found somehow to fix in the illiterate's mind the story he has learned.[176]

Several things need to be kept in mind in the preparation of stories for primary oral communicators:

- Story complexity - Hence the need for simplifying many stories with difficult-to-visualize numerical detail and a confusing plethora of proper names of characters and geographical places.

- Story context - The sequence before and after stories that frame a story or give perspective.

- Story repetition - The need for repetition by the storyer and by listeners during the storying sessions - Oral learners learn from repetition and from retelling the stories or exercising them.

- Group Story - The phenomenon of the "group story" in which the group possesses the story and to some extent self-corrects the stories that changes creep into (There are certain "story-keepers" among many people groups.)[177]

Over time it will be necessary to have someone periodically refresh the Bible stories to correct any drift in the stories. An alternative is to provide suitable recordings of the stories that can be reviewed among the listeners to maintain a baseline for preserving the stories.

Continuity Strategies

One of the most crucial factors in ensuring that Bible storying results in churches is the presence of continuity strategies. Steven King expresses this concern when he states:

> Some attention needs to be given to the continuing discipleship aspect. Oral learners need to continue to learn the Word of God. I have seen the majority of our work in CBS focused on getting churches started. When the community does not read then some strategy

must be implemented that provides a means for the community to "self feed" without depending on the missionaries.[178]

In addition to the need for ongoing discipleship, there are several components that can be a part of a Bible storyer's continuity strategy. These include shadow storying, establishing accountability, avoiding dependence, and planning a timely exit.

Shadow Storying

Missionaries who have worked in contexts where church planting movements have emerged have developed the concept of "shadow pastoring." By this they mean that the missionaries are initially involved in leading people to Christ and then training in such a way that the local leaders assume the leadership for the congregations that emerge. From this perspective "Shadow Storying" means that the local leaders become the storyers early in the Bible Storying process. Steve Flook gives an example of this:

> Also another key factor is the instructor or missionary must make every effort in staying behind the scenes. A foreigner (American Missionary) must never be the spot light of any presentation when teaching the CBS strategy to nationals. First train a national in private then allow the national to present the CBS strategies along with you assisting him. The nationals and people who you are training or trying to reach must see that they have the "ownership" of what is being presented instead of them seeing an intelligent, wealthy, and arrogant American teaching the class (World View of most foreigners of Americans). Quickly push and pass the responsibility and ownership of CBS to the people from the very beginning, starting on the first day you arrive. Encourage them by reassuring them that the Holy Spirit will strengthen and enable them to do the CBS and that it is not dependent on how well they speak or remember the stories. Again the success of the CBS strategy is

107

directly related to the environment in which it is presented. Therefore the environment that must be created first is an environment of Dependency upon God and his resources which is Christ, God's Word, Prayer and the Holy Spirit. And the second environment which must be created simultaneously with the first is an environment of responsibility, high accountability and expectations. When these types of environments are created along with the CBS strategy then I believe we will see more multiplication and many more CPM's. Why? Because God gets the Glory and the focus shifts from man and his abilities to God and his abilities. Let's turn it over to God and He will do it! To Him be the GLORY![179]

The approach that Jackson Day has developed and employs facilitates the accountability that Flook emphasizes. Day utilizes a three-step approach to apprenticeship training. He describes it in the following manner:

- Modeling: the master performs a task with the apprentice observing. Some explanation is given to help the apprentice understand how the task is being done. The master shows the apprentice how to do the task.

- Coaching: the master becomes a mentor who coaches the apprentice through different activities necessary to do the task. When coaching, the master observes the apprentice carrying out a task and offers hints, feedback, modeling, reminders, and new tasks aimed at improving his performance. Coaching is the process of overseeing the apprentice's learning.

- Fading: as the apprentice improves his skills, the master decreases his coaching and gives the apprentice more and more responsibility. The apprentice receives responsibilities away from the watchful eye of the master.[180]

As Flook and Day have discovered, accountability on the part of the local people has contributed significantly toward the effectiveness of their CBS efforts.

Establishing accountability

Building accountability into the Bible Storying process is absolutely essential in ensuring that churches are started. In some instances an enormous amount of work has gone into some CBS efforts but with few if any lasting results. It is not until local people buy into the effort and accept it as theirs that lasting results can become evident. Flook strongly stresses this when he states:

> What makes the CBS strategy work is the type of atmosphere that is created by the missionary or person who has presented it. An atmosphere of high accountability, responsibility, and high expectations must be created for the CBS strategy to work. Seriousness must be placed on the process of CBS by the instructor at all times with high accountability when teaching and discipling a person. Everyone that we instructed and discipled in the CBS strategy knew that they were responsible and accountable to God first and to us for sharing the stories every week with their family, friends, and neighbors. [181]

Flook sees this accountability as requiring more that a commitment to a specific evangelistic strategy. For him, it requires a commitment of a person's life. He explains:

> Along with the CBS principles and strategies we also taught our people what it meant to be responsible and committed to Christ in all areas of their lives and not only to CBS . How to plan and set goals and how to be responsible in fulfilling what they said they would do or promise. CBS involves so much more than only training a person to remember and share the Bible Stories that they had learned in chronological order. Each person has to be personally discipled by someone in all areas of their life. If a person we were training repeatedly had a difficult time in showing up for his discipleship training or had a reoccurring problem with showing up on

time, then we would prayerfully begin looking at training and working with someone else. [182]

Avoiding dependency

Dependency can be another factor that delays church planting in connection with Bible Storying. It can be an unintended by product of a concerted effort to establish meaningful relationships with the people we are trying to reach. LaNette Thompson alludes to this in her evaluation of Bible Storying strategies. She explains:

> Because it may take a long time to do the Evangelism Track, we can build such good relationships with the people that we become a part of their network and dependency results. We may feel responsible if they are persecuted. They learn to depend upon us. There is no impetus for them to bring others to Christ.[183]

Timely exit

A timely exit by the church planter significantly impacts the entire movement among a people group. Either leaving too soon or staying too long can affect the timeliness of the exit LaNette Thompson describes the danger of leaving too soon:

> I called the missionary who had been over the work and was told that their concern was that after the fast track of stories, the missionary pulled out too soon without adequate discipleship or leadership training, and that contributed to the attrition rate, not the storying method itself.[184]

Thompson makes an excellent point here. **One cannot blame a method if it has not been implemented wisely.** This applies to any type of Christian ministry. Speaking specifically about church planting, whatever methodology is employed, if it is not implemented correctly and in a timely fashion there is a very high probability that it is not going to be effective. If that is the case, it is not the method but the way it is used that bears the blame for ineffectiveness.

I had a similar concern in South Asia. Many of the young men who were in my CBS training in Bangladesh and some parts of India needed storying first of all so that they themselves could be discipled and so they could understand about salvation and why Jesus had to suffer and die. Then the training in storying had to equip them with stories and competency to lead a discussion of the stories as they gathered groups. Limited funds and administrative changes made it impossible for me to follow through with my plans. What they needed next was training on using the narratives in a church worship service. [185]

There were many situations where people from other villages visited storying sites and heard the stories and then took the stories back to their own people. I did once experience the visit of three men from a large community who heard about the Bible Storying being conducted in a nearby city. The men came near the end of the storying and later told the group that they had heard about this same Jesus from a man who came to their place for one day and told them and then left. Now they wanted to have someone to come and tell all of the story of this Jesus so their people could hear it.

An interesting note is that the re-emergence of Chronological Bible Teaching came about because of the premature exit of a missionary family who had worked among a tribal group on the island of Palawan in the Philippines. The missionary was still learning the local language and had apparently planted a church or churches among the people who did not really understand salvation. When New Tribes missionary Trevor McIlwain realized the lost condition of these "church-goers" and when he tried to correct their belief by teaching, he found the people resistant. When McIlwain realized that the people had no concept of "lostness" he began teaching chronologically from Creation through the Old Testament stories to teach about "lostness" so the people would be ready to accept salvation. [186]

A timely exit requires that the Bible storyer stay long enough to enable converts to become grounded in the faith yet not so long that local leaders are not developed. There is no hard and fast rule that specifies the amount of time a storyer needs to continue to relate to the new group. One can establish some indicators. Some of these could include:

- The genuine conversion of some individuals within a people group;

- Indication that some of these believers are progressing in their discipleship to the extent that they have an understanding of what it means to be a follower of Jesus;

- The emergence of some leaders who are willing to be trained and to assume responsibility;

- A sense of community on the part of the believers;

- An indication that these believers are willing to function as a congregation in their local setting.

On the other hand, some church planters have erred by staying too long. The church planter should not limit the development of the local leaders by staying too long. Local leaders must be allowed to assume leadership without being overshadowed by the church planter. One of the best resources for planning for a timely exit is Tom Steffen's book, *Passing the Baton*.[187] **Bible storyers would be wise to follow his advice of planning the exit strategy before the storying process is begun.**

There is a sense in which a "timely exit" should include a "timely transition" to ensure that the people group has access to enough Bible to develop a healthy church life (the whole counsel of God – Acts 20:27). This transition should be from the immediate church planting situation to the ongoing coaching of a people group movement. This, obviously, would call for a role change on the part of the original Bible storyer from an initiator and trainer to a coach.

Depending on the Holy Spirit

Underlying everything that is done in Bible Storying must be deep and total dependence upon the work of the Holy Spirit. Undoubtedly many storyers agree with Steve Flook that dependence upon the work of the Holy Spirit is absolutely essential for effectiveness in any type of Christian ministry including Chronological Bible Storying. Steve explains:

> The contributing factor to seeing reproducibility in church planting where we were was the fact that CBS strategy contributed to the process of creating an atmosphere of dependency on God and His resources (Christ, His Word, Prayer, and the Holy Spirit) instead of on man and his resources. Therefore, the people were not dependent upon a missionary or an outsider in order to continue the reproducibility process, but were dependent upon God and His resources. Even though CBS is a very effective tool in reaching people, we must teach the students that the key elements empowering this CBS strategy are Prayer and the Holy Spirit. As with any tool I believe the key to seeing more multiplication in church planting is by creating an **environment of dependency upon God and his resources which are Christ, his Word, Prayer, and the Holy Spirit.** And this can only be done through modeling and discipling this type of environment to the person whom we are teaching the CBS to. Without dependency on God and his resources then all we have created is a thin shallow dependency on the strategy of Storying which will only last for a short while. [188]

Dependence upon the work of the Holy Spirit includes dependence upon the timing of the Holy Spirit. Sometimes I suspected it was not that peoples' time to have church. They were friendly and listened, but the message did not stick or motivate them to church. There are times when a significant amount of seed sowing is needed before people become receptive to the Gospel message. It is during these times that storyers need to continue to share God's Word with the expectation that the Holy Spirit will touch the hearts of people and bring many to repentance.

While on the one hand we should do everything possible to sow the Gospel seed abundantly, on the other hand we should be aware that it may not be the Holy Spirit's timing for a great harvest with this particular group. While we may appear to fail to plant a church immediately, I firmly believe that we never go wrong in telling the Bible stories so that in God's time fruit may result. We have diligently tried to emphasize, and you will hear us say this again and again, "don't be locked into an inflexible system when the Spirit opens doors earlier than expected."

An understanding of the cultural background of a people group and of Bible storying principles are is absolutely essential for the type of Bible storying that leads to church planting. Having said all of this, however, it must be pointed out that there are times when the Holy Spirit (through dreams, miracles, and other divine manifestations) cuts right through the layers of erroneous worldview perceptions and prepares the hearts of the people to receive the message of Jesus. Storying church planters, therefore, should always be sensitive to the work of the Holy Spirit in their own lives as well as the lives of the members of the people group. What we have shared here are some guidelines. These guidelines are helpful in designing strategies for reaching people groups with the gospel and starting churches among them. Like the apostle Paul, however, they should always be willing to be led by the Holy Spirit and go to Macedonia even if their original plans were to go to Bithynia (Acts 16:7-9).

Conclusion

In this chapter we have focused on the strategies that are needed to ensure that Bible storying efforts result in the establishment of churches. These include: 1) Initial strategies; 2) Church starting strategies; 3) Training strategies; 4) and Continuity strategies. The last of the continuity strategies indicates that it is absolutely essential to depend on the work of the Holy Spirit. For assistance with the implementation of these factors see Appendices I and J. We now turn our attention to the challenge of selecting the Bible stories for effective church planting.

Chapter 4:
Selecting Bible Stories

The book of God's revelation, with its witness to Christ which has come down to us in human language, points to a person and to a story – with all the varied nuances and aspects of personal and community life.

H.R. Weber

We used storying to plant a church and to initiate work in several new locations that the nationals eventually developed into churches.

Donald Barger

The centerpiece of the Bible Storying approach is obviously the stories that are selected and shared with a particular people group. These accounts will be instrumental in people coming to a saving knowledge of Jesus Christ, following him in discipleship, gathering into congregations, training leaders, and continuing to grow and to multiply as Christians in their communities. Because of these important goals those of us involved in Chronological Bible Storying talk about the various tracks: 1) Evangelism; 2) Discipleship; 3) Church Planting; 4) Leadership Training, etc.[189]

The value of these tracks is that they help the storyer focus on the specific aim for the people group at a specific time in their development. There is a sense in which these are sequential. It is logical to focus first on leading people to Christ. On the other hand, these tracks often overlap. For example, in the Evangelism Track a foundation can be laid for the other tracks. This can especially be true of the Church Planting Track. In other words, as people are evangelized through storying a foundation can be laid for them to begin to think early in the process about their need to gather together to worship, observe the ordinances, continue in their discipleship, minister to one another, and carry out the other functions of a church found in the New Testament, especially Acts 2:40-27.

What we will attempt to do in this chapter is to highlight stories in the Evangelism Track that are especially suitable for preparing for the Church Planting Track. This approach will ensure that church planting is an integral part of the storying process and not an afterthought once the Evangelism Track has been completed. The goal is that the people will begin to think about their need to form into congregations as they are hearing the stories related to their salvation. Following the segment where we highlight some of the stories that are better suited to lay the church planting foundation, we will suggest a Church Planting Story Set that can serve as a guide for the development of a church planting strategy for the specific people groups among which the storyers are going to work. In light of the fact that there are numerous excellent story sets for the Evangelism Track, we are not going to develop yet another story set. Instead we are going to suggest some of the stories that lend themselves the best for laying this foundation.

Stories From the Evangelism Track

When these stories are told during the Evangelism Track they can lay a foundation for church starting. These stories can be drawn from both the Old Testament and the New Testament. The following ideas need to be emphasized in the story and in the dialog session:

Stories from the Old Testament

The Following Jesus discipleship series developed by Dr Avery Willis and a team of eight specialists has excellent suggestions for sowing the seeds for church planting even while Old Testament stories are being shared.[190]

- Tabernacle of the Congregation
- Solomon's Temple Consecrated and Dedicated
- Worshipping God Is Not Limited to a Building[191]

Stories from the New Testament

- Jesus Sending the Delivered Demoniac Back To His Family (Matthew 8:28; Mark 5:1; Luke 8:26-39)
    - o Biblical principle: The importance of sharing the Good News with family and friends
- Sending the 12 – Finding Person of Peace (Matthew 10)
    - o Biblical principle: The importance of finding persons of peace
- Jesus: "I will build my church" (Matthew 16: 13-20)
    - o Biblical principle: It is Jesus who builds His church
    - o Church Discipline (Matthew 18:15-20)
    - o Concept: How to serve Jesus taught of serving him in a community of believers
- Cleansing of the Temple (Matthew 21: 12; Mark 11:15-17)
    - o Concept: The church is God's house of prayer
- Jesus Institutes the Lord's Supper (Matthew 26: 17-29; Mark 14:22)
    - o Concept: The Lord's Supper is a part of the worship experience of the church
- Christ's Prayer for the Church (John 17: 1-26)
    - o Concept: The followers of Jesus are in the world but not of the world
    - o Concept: Jesus is interested in the well-being of his followers
- Jesus Giving the Great Commission (Matthew 28: 1-20)
    - o Concept: The disciples of Jesus are to make disciples of people groups in all the nations of the world[192]

Many Bible stories can be used to share these principles and concepts and the storyer needs to feel free to select the stories that are most useful and appropriate in a given setting.

Chronology of Acts as a Church Planting Model

To our knowledge one of the earliest attempts at establishing a clear path from Bible storying to church planting was the work done by Dr. Jim Slack entitled: "Chronology of Acts As Church Planting Model." In it he suggested the utilization of following stories:

- **Story 1:** Going to the "*ta ethne*" as a fulfillment of the Great Commission (Acts 1-2:1-13)

- **Story 2:** Preaching of Peter and establishment of the first Church in Jerusalem (Acts 2: 14-47)

- **Story 3:** Witness and Healing In The Community, Including Opposition The Disciples Face From The Religious Community. (3:1-4:21)

- **Story 4:** Testimonies Of Deliverance Shared With Church. (4:22-37)

- **Story 5:** God Deals With Dishonesty and A Breach In Unity Within The Church. (5:1-16)

- **Story 6:** The Early Believers Face Persecution and The Church Grows. (5:17-42)

- **Story 7:** The Jerusalem Church Faces A Racial Crisis And The Leaders Leading The Congregation To Solve The Crisis. (Acts 6:1-7)

- **Story 8:** The Local Church Leader Stephen Witnesses and Stands Up For His Faith and Is Stoned. (Acts 6:8-8:4)

- **Story 9:** Another "Deacon's" Ministry Beyond Waiting On Tables—Philip (Acts 8:1-40)

- **Story 10:** God Brings An "Enemy" Into The Kingdom And Into The Church (Acts 9:1-43)

118

- **Story 11:** Peter Is "Forced" By God To Go To The "*Ta Ethne*" (Cornelius, The Roman) (10:1-48)

- **Story 12:** The Jerusalem Church Questions Peter's Actions, Then Accepts *Ta Ethne* (Gentiles) Into the Church. (Acts 11:1-18)

- **Story 13:** A New Local Church Emerges In Antioch And A Look At Relations Between Local Churches-- Antioch and Jerusalem. (11:19-30)[193]

These Bible stories from the book of Acts provide a solid foundation as well as an excellent model for church planting. As we present the following story set we are aware that we are standing on the shoulders of Dr. Jim Slack who has always maintained a strong commitment to church planting through the utilization of Chronological Bible Storying strategies.

Church Planting Story Set

In this segment we are going to develop a church planting story set based on the book of Acts. As we do it, however, we need to make it clear that we are not positing this as a generic story set that applies to every setting without modification. In keeping with what we have said earlier, it will be absolutely essential for the process that we have suggested for the development of shell models to be followed here. This involves the following steps:

- Review worldview characteristics of your people group;

- Indicate the basic Bible truth you want to emphasize with each story;

- Select the stories (with scripture references) that communicate that Bible truth more clearly and contextually;

- For each story write pre-story questions;

- Plan the post-story activities to ensure that the listeners have truly learned the lessons in that story and are ready to apply them;

- Develop a brief outline for each story indicating the main points (scenes) of the story;

- Write out the story fully;

- Tell the story and learn from the response of the people;

- Make the necessary modifications that will improve the story in that particular setting.

Two further explanations. First, even though most of the stories in this story set will be from the book of Acts, this is not essentially a "storying through the book of Acts" story set. There are many stories from the book of Acts that we will not use in this set. These can be included later in an advanced church planting story set or in another set (e.g., Discipleship). **The aim of this story set is to take the people through a direct and expeditious line of church planting instances in the book of Acts**.

As a matter of fact, even this story set can be abbreviated if needed to get the people group involved in church planting as soon as possible. The second explanation is that we are essentially going to share a series of paraphrased stories in this story set. The main goal is to be in a position to cover the most important concepts and principles in these stories in order to establish a foundation for church planting in a particular people group setting.[194]

The Ascension of Jesus
(Acts 1)

Pre-Story Dialog

We have already heard the story of how Jesus died on the cross. We have also heard the story of how God brought Jesus back to life three days after he was buried. Today we are going to hear the story of how Jesus went up into heaven and what he told his disciples to do. As you hear the story listen to see what you learn about how Jesus proved that he had come back to life, what he told his followers that they should do, how he went up into heaven, and what the angels said about Jesus. This is a story from God's Word.

The Story

After Jesus was brought back to life by God, he appeared to his disciples on many different occasions over a period of forty days. When he did appear to his disciples, he talked to them about the Kingdom of God. He then told them:

"Go back to Jerusalem and wait there until the Father gives you the Spirit that I told you he has promised to give you. John baptized with water but in a few days you will be baptized with the Holy Spirit."

When his disciples heard this they asked: *"Lord are you going to free Israel so it becomes as an independent nation again?"* Jesus explained to them that this information is not something they needed to know. God is the one who knows when this will happen. But the Holy Spirit is going to come upon you and give you power. Then you will tell everyone about me in the city of Jerusalem, throughout the province of Judea, in the neighboring province of Samaria, and everywhere in the world."

Right after Jesus said this as they were still watching he started going up into the sky until a cloud covered him and they could not see him any longer. He disappeared but the disciples kept looking up into the sky.

All of a sudden two men dressed in white robes appeared among them and said: *"Why are you still standing here and looking up to the sky? Jesus has gone into heaven and some day he is going to come back just like you saw him go up."*

Post-Story Dialog

Among the other important lessons in this story, make sure that you help them to clearly grasp the concept that Jesus expects them to tell their family, friends, neighbors, and others that He died and was brought back to life to they can have an abundant life. Another point to make is that Jesus is coming back and we need to obey to tell people about him.

Becoming a Church
(Acts 2:1 - 47)

Pre-Story Dialog

Last time we heard the story about what Jesus told his disciples before he went up into heaven. Today we are going to hear the story of how the disciples obeyed Jesus and how they got together as a group and formed a church. As I tell the story, please listen very carefully to find out how they were filled with the Holy Spirit, what the Apostle Peter told the people, and what they did when they got together as a church.

The Story

This is a story from God's Word. After Jesus went up into heaven the apostles went back to Jerusalem and had a prayer meeting in the upstairs room of a house. While they were there praying for many days, about 120 of them, all of a sudden felt a strong, loud wind that filled the house. The Holy Spirit came into their hearts and they started speaking languages that they had never learned before. People who had come from many different countries were very surprised because they heard the disciples speak their languages. Some were wondering what this meant but others thought the believers were drunk.

The Apostle Peter then stood up and told them that they were seeing what the Prophet Joel had predicted many years before. Peter then told them that Jesus, the Son of God, had come and worked many miracles among them but they had refused to believe and yelled out that Jesus should die on the cross. But this Jesus came back to life and was taken up by God into heaven.

When the people heard this many of them felt very sorry and they asked Peter: *"What should we do."* And Peter told them *"turn back to God and be baptized in the name of Jesus and then you will receive the Holy Spirit."* On that day 3,000 people believed in Jesus and were baptized.

That same day, those who were baptized became a part of the Church of Jesus. All of these joined with the other believers and every day they spent their time learning from the apostles and they became like a family. They shared with one another what they had, praised God together, they prayed for each other, and received God's answering miracles. They ate together and observed the Lord's supper in the Temple and in their homes with a lot of joy and thankfulness. All of the people in their communities liked them and because of the power of God, new people believed in Christ every day.

Post-Story Dialog

Among the other things be sure to dialog with them about the things the people did when they came together in their church. Highlight in the story the things the church did: 1) Sharing the good news (v. 40); 2) Baptizing new believers (v. 41); 3) Learning and following the doctrines of the apostles (42); 4) Having fellowship with one another (v. 42); 5) Having the Lord's Supper (v. 42); 6) Praying (v. 42); 7) Helping one another (vv. 44, 45); 8) Praising God in the temple and in their homes (vv. 46,47); 9) Creating goodwill with all the people (v. 47); 10) Receiving new believers every day (v. 47).

Help the new believers to begin to think of how they need to start getting together to begin living as a church.

Selecting People to Serve
In the Church
(Acts 6)

Pre-Story Dialog

Last time we heard the story of the way in which the believers in Jesus Christ got together and formed a church. Today we want to hear the story of how this church selected people to serve the church. As I tell the story, please listen to find out what some of the different activities in the church are, how the congregation picked people to serve the people in the church, what qualities the servants in the church needed to have, and what happened after the servants were given the responsibility of serving.

The Story

This is a story from God's Word. Sometime after the church had been formed there began to be some complaints among the members. Those who spoke another language began to complain that their widows were not being given the same amount of food every day as those who spoke their native tongue. Now when the apostles heard this they got all the people together and said to them: *"We should not be giving up speaking about God's Word to serve tables. Find seven men who are respected, wise, and filled with the Holy Spirit and ask them to serve the tables so we can continue speaking about God's Word."*

The people in the church thought that this was a good idea so they chose a man named Stephen who had a lot of faith and was filled with the Holy Spirit. They then chose Philip and five other men and brought them to the apostles. The apostles then placed their hands on their heads and prayed for them and asked the blessing of God for them as they did the work that they were chosen to do.

The way in which these men served the church was so good that many people in the city became very interested in hearing the Word of God. Even leaders from the religion of the Jews decided to become followers of Jesus.

Post-Story Dialog

Be sure to emphasize that: 1) The new church faced a problem (vv. 1, 2); 2) The church selected men who were honest, full of the Holy Spirit, had wisdom, and were willing to serve. Lead them in a discussion of the different ministries that are needed in the church. Help them to see how the church members participated in selecting the servants. Help them to be aware that when people follow what God wants them to do, many people are willing to hear the teachings about God and become followers of Jesus.

Suffering Persecution
(Acts 6:8 – 7:60)

It may or may not be necessary to include this story in the Church Planting Story Set for your people group at this time. If there is persecution going on or if there is a need to underscore the necessity to make a clean break with the people group's traditional religion, this story can help.

Pre-Story Dialog

Last time we heard the story of how the servants for the church were chosen in order to help solve the problem that the church was facing. You will remember that one of the servants was named Stephen. In our story we are going to hear today, I want you to listen very closely to find out what Stephen told the Jewish leaders who were against Jesus, what the religious leaders did, and what happened to Stephen.

The Story

Not long after Stephen was chosen as a servant of the church the people noticed that God had given Stephen power to tell people about Jesus and to do many miracles. Some of the Jewish leaders who were against Jesus started arguing with Stephen but he had so much wisdom from God that the leaders could not win their arguments. The religious leaders then decided to get some bad men to tell lies about Stephen. This caused many of the people to get angry with Stephen and they dragged him in front of a council. While they were telling lies about Stephen his face was with the glory of God.

Stephen then told them the story of their people. He spoke to them about the way God had called Abraham, how Joseph had become a leader in Egypt, how Moses freed the people from their slavery in Egypt by bringing them out, and leading them to the land God had chosen for them.

He also told them about when Moses went up to the mountain to receive God's laws the people got tired of waiting for him and made a statue of a calf out of gold and worshipped the calf as if it were a god. He told them that God became angry with them because they were worshiping idols.

Stephen also told them: *"You have always been stubborn. You have always fought against the Holy Spirit. You have always been against the prophet that God has sent you. And when God sent his own Son you turned against him and killed him."*

Well when the members of the council heard this they became very angry. But Stephen was full of the Holy Spirit. He looked up into the heavens and said: *"I see heaven open and Jesus standing at the right hand of God."* When they heard this, the religious leaders dragged Stephen and started throwing stones at him. While they were doing this a young man named Saul was taking care of their coats.

While Stephen was being stoned to death he cried out: *"Jesus, please receive me."* And he also shouted: *"Jesus, do not punish them for what they have done."* After he said this he died. Then men who were followers of Jesus buried Stephen and were very sad.

Post-Story Dialog

Lead the people in the dialog to understand that there are times when the followers of Jesus have to suffer persecution. If the people have an animistic background, help them to know how much God hates idolatry. It may be helpful to talk about the way in which the followers of Jesus can help one another when they suffer persecution. You can also lead them in a discussion about the way in which Stephen forgave those who were putting him to death. You can also talk about the way in which Jesus received Stephen when he died.

Sharing the Good News with Strangers (Acts 8: 1-36)

One of the greatest needs related to church planting is that of helping new believers to know that they have a privilege and a responsibility to share the gospel with others. The story of Philip can help inspire people to witness even to people who are enemies or strangers.

Pre-Story Dialog

Last time you heard the story of Stephen. Today I am going to tell you the story of another one of the men who were chosen as servants of God. His name was Philip. When you hear the story, please see if you can find out how Philip felt about sharing the good news about Jesus with the Samaritans who were enemies of Philip's Jewish people group. Also listen to find out how the people in Samaria responded when Philip told them about Jesus and the changes this made in their lives. When you hear the story try to find out if these new believers were baptized like the believers in Jerusalem. Also see if you can discover if Philip obeyed the Holy Spirit.

The Story

After Stephen was buried many of the leaders of the Jewish religion who hated Jesus started persecuting the believers. This persecution caused many of the believers to run away to other cities. Philip decided to go to Samaria to tell the people about Jesus. When he got there, large crowds started to gather because they wanted to hear what he was saying and to see the miracles God was working through Philip. Many of the people who had evil spirits were healed and everyone in that city was very happy because of what was happening. When they believed what Philip was telling them about Jesus, they were baptized.

One day an angel of God appeared to Philip and said to him: *"I want you to leave and go to a road in the desert."* Philip obeyed God and went to the desert. While he was walking in the desert, a chariot came along the road. In the chariot was an Ethiopian who was chief treasurer of the queen of the country of Ethiopia. This official had gone to Jerusalem to worship and was now returning home. As he was traveling he was reading aloud the scroll that the prophet Isaiah wrote. The Holy Spirit told Philip: *"Run and get close to the chariot."* When Philip did, he heard asked the man *"do you understand what you are reading?"* The man answered, *"I cannot understand it unless someone explains it to me."* The man was reading the part that says: *"He was led like a sheep to be killed and did not say a word."* Philip then explained to him that this message of the prophet was about Jesus. Philip explained to him that Jesus came to save those who believe in him.

As they were traveling, the man said: *"Look there's some water, why can I not be baptized?"* So they stopped the chariot and went down into the water and Philip baptized him. After that the man went on his way and was very happy.

Post-Story Dialog

Depending on the needs of the people group some key concepts can be brought out from the story. 1) The importance of sharing the good news with others, even our enemies. 2) The change that receiving Christ can make (in both cases they were filled with joy). 3) The importance of being baptized after believing in Christ. Note: In this story we did not deal with Simon the sorcerer. If your people group is animistic, this part of the story can be very useful to underscore God's repudiation of this practice, God's power over evil, and the need to make a clear-cut separation from all magical practices.

An Enemy Becomes an Ally
(Acts 9: 1-19)

The conversion of Paul, an enemy of the church, and his becoming the most prolific church planter is a powerful story that should inspire future church planters. While there are many facets to Paul's ministry, highlighting his church planting commitment and strategy can be very useful in this story set.

Pre-Story Dialog

Have you ever known someone that you think will never become a believer? Today I am going to tell you a story about someone who was an enemy of the church and persecuted the believers. As you listen to this story try to find out how this man "Saul" who later changed his name to "Paul" had an encounter with Jesus. Listen carefully to what Jesus told him. Also listen carefully to the way Paul answered Jesus.

Try to find out how a man called Ananias helped Paul. You will remember that Paul was so much against the Christian believers that he held and guarded the clothing of the religious leaders who threw stones at Stephen and killed him.

The Story

Paul continued to threaten the followers of Jesus. He went to the leaders of the Jewish leaders and asked them for letters to go to the city of Damascus. He wanted to go there to arrest the followers of Jesus and bring them back to Jerusalem to put them in jail.

When Paul had gotten close to Damascus all of a sudden a very bright light from heaven surrounded him. He fell to the ground and he heard a voice that said to him: *"Paul, Paul, why are you persecuting me?"* But Paul did not know who was talking to him so he asked: *"Who are you."* And the voice answered, *"I am Jesus the one that you are fighting against. I want you to get up and go to the city and there they will tell you what you need to do."*

The men who were traveling with Paul could not say anything. They heard the voice but did not see anything. When Paul got up from the ground he opened his eyes but could not see. So the men who were traveling with him had to lead him by the hand to Damascus and for three days he did not drink nor eat anything.

Now in the city of Damascus there was a believer of Jesus and his name was Ananias. God spoke to him and told him: *"Get up and go to the house of Judas which is on Straight street and there you will find a man named Paul. He is praying and has seen a vision. In his vision he saw a man named Ananias who came to him, put his hands on him and he could see again."*

But Ananias said: *"Lord, many people have told me all the terrible things this man has done to your followers in Jerusalem."* The Lord said to him: *"Go, because I have chosen him to tell many strangers and kings and the people of Israel about me."*

So Ananias went to the house where Paul was staying. When he got there he placed his hands on Paul and said to him: *"Paul, Jesus who appeared to you on the road has sent me. He wants you to see again and to be filled with his Holy Spirit."* Immediately things that were like coverings fell from Paul's eyes and he was able to see again. He then got up and was baptized. He stayed for several days there in Damascus with other believers and very soon started to tell the people that Jesus is the Son of God. Many people who heard him asked: *"Isn't he the man who fought against the followers of Jesus and came here to take them to prison?"*

But he told the Jewish people with a lot of power and emotion that Jesus was the Son of God. Some of the religious leaders became so angry that they began to make plans to kill Paul. Their plan was to guard the gate of the city so Paul could not escape. One night the believers let Paul down in a large basket over the city wall.

Paul went from there to Jerusalem and he tried to get together with the believers but they were afraid of Paul and did not believe that he had become a follower of Jesus. There was a believer named Barnabas (his name means one who encourages) and he took Paul to the apostles and explained to them how Jesus had appeared to Paul. Paul then started telling the Jews that Jesus was the Son of God and they became so angry they tried to kill Paul. To protect him the believers took Paul to another city and from there he returned to the city where he was born, Tarsus.

Post-Story Dialog

In the dialog, deal with the questions suggested in the pre-story dialog. Emphasize to power of God to change the lives of even people who are fighting against Jesus. Also emphasize the points in the story that strengthen the idea of people gathering into congregations. Show how people who are strong believers like Ananias can help new believers to get close to God. This story can also be a place to emphasize once again that new believers need to be baptized like Paul was after he believed in Jesus.

Starting a Church at Antioch
(Act 8:1; Acts 11: 19, 20; Acts 13:1-3)

Pre-Story Dialog

The other day we told you the story of how the Church in Jerusalem was started. Then we told you the story of how Stephen was killed and there was a strong persecution against the believers in Jesus. This persecution caused many of the believers in Jesus to leave and go to other cities.

Today I am going to tell you the story of how the people who fled to the city of Antioch started a church there. As you listen to the story, listen to find out the people with whom these Christian refugees shared the good news about Jesus first. Then pay attention to find out if they spoke about Jesus to people of other people groups. As you continue to listen to the story see if you can find out if the people in this church were willing to let their leaders go to other places to start other churches.

The Story

After people who refused to believe in Jesus killed Stephen, many others started to be cruel to the believers who lived in Jerusalem. This forced many of the believers to go to other cities. Well, one of the groups of believers went to the city of Antioch. When they got there they found many people who were of their own Jewish people group and spoke their language. The believers from Jerusalem then started talking to these people about Jesus and many of them became believers in Jesus.

After this response, other believers came from other cities and they began to talk about Jesus with a group of Greeks who had a different culture and a different language. As a result of this witness, many Greeks also believed in Jesus and became a part of that new church. Because of this God was very pleased with them.

After a while the members of the church in Jerusalem sent a man named Barnabas to encourage the new believers in the church at Antioch. After Barnabas had been there for a while he went to Tarsus and brought Paul to help him with the work at the church. The two of them worked in that church for a year. During that time a prophet came and told them that there was going to be a drought in Jerusalem and the followers of Jesus would suffer hunger. The members of the church then decided to take up an offering and send it to their brothers and sisters in the church in Jerusalem.

One day after the members of the church had gone a long time without eating and had spent a lot of time praying and praising God, the Holy Spirit said to them: "*Set aside Barnabas and Paul for a very important job I have for them.*" The members of the church then placed their hands on Barnabas and Paul, gave them their blessing, and sent them away to do God's will. Barnabas and Paul then started their journey to many cities where they started churches.

Post-Story Dialog

Select some of the questions we listed above and help the people think about the answers. Focus on the fact that this refugee group was immediately willing to tell people from their own people group about Jesus. Help them in the discussion to become aware of the fact that this group was willing to tell people of other people groups about Jesus. Help them to find out that this church was willing to let their leaders go to other cities to tell people about Jesus and to start churches. Help them to see that it was the will of God for Barnabas and Paul to go to other cities to start churches. Help them to see how the members of the church in Antioch were willing to give money to help their brothers and sisters in the church in Jerusalem.

Starting a Church in Lystra
(Acts 14: 8-24)

Pre-Story Dialog

Last time I told you the story of how the church at Antioch was willing to obey the Holy Spirit and let Barnabas and Paul leave so they could start churches in many other cities. Today I am going to tell you the story of how they started a church in the city of Lystra. As you listen to this story, try to find answers to these questions: 1) What made the people in this city want to hear Barnabas and Paul? 2) Who did the people think Barnabas and Paul were? 3) Did Paul suffer because he told people about Jesus? 4) What did Paul do when he returned to Lystra? 5) Do we need people to lead in our churches today?

The Story

After Paul and Barnabas left the church at Antioch they went to many cities telling people about Jesus. When they got to the city of Lystra they saw a man who had never been able to walk because he was born cripple. This man listened to Paul speak about Jesus. Paul noticed that this man had enough faith to be healed so he looked at him and shouted: *"Stand up."* Immediately the man jumped up and started walking.

When the people saw this they said: *"These are gods that have put on a human body and have come down to visit us."* The people then gave Barnabas the name Zeus and Paul the name Hermes, the names of two of their gods. The temple of their god Zeus was close by and the priests and the crowds wanted to offer sacrifices to Paul and Barnabas. The priests then brought bulls and flowers to the city gates to offer them as sacrifices to Paul and Barnabas.

When Paul and Barnabas saw this they tore their clothes to let the people know that they were very upset. They then ran to the crowds and started shouting: *"We are humans just like you. Do not worship us. Worship God who made the sky, the earth, the sea, and everything in them. It is God who makes rain come down from heaven and makes the crops grow. He is the one that gives you food and makes your hearts happy."*

While they were doing this, Jewish leaders from Antioch came and made the crowds angry at Paul and Barnabas. The people hit Paul with many stones and dragged him out of the city because they thought he was dead. But the people who had believed in Jesus picked Paul up and brought him back into the city. The next day Paul and Barnabas went to another city.

After some time Paul and Barnabas went back into the city of Lystra and encouraged the followers of Jesus and told them to continue to be faithful to him. They told them: *"We have to suffer before we go to be in God's kingdom."* While they were in Lystra, Paul and Barnabas chose leaders for the church. Then they spent a lot of time praying that the Lord would give his blessing to these leaders. After this Paul and Barnabas went to other cities to tell them about Jesus.

Post-Story Dialog

Select the questions from the Pre-Story Dialog that fit the best and use them for this part of the dialog. If there are animistic tendencies, it will be helpful to stress Paul and Barnabas' response the intention of the people to offer them sacrifices. It is important in this dialog to stress the importance of choosing leaders for the church.

Starting a Church in Philippi
(Composite Story Acts 16: 11-38)

Pre-Story Dialog

Last time we told you the story of how the refugees from Jerusalem started a church in the city of Antioch. We also told you that Barnabas and Paul served God in that church until the Holy Spirit chose them to go to other cities to lead people to believe in Christ and to get together as churches.

Today we are going to tell you the story of how Paul went to Philippi and started a church. As I tell the story, listen very closely to see if you can find out how Paul got to meet people (persons of peace) and how he told them about Jesus. I also want you to hear the story very carefully to see if after they helped people to believe in Jesus they got them together in groups or churches. Also try to find out if when the new believers decided to be baptized. After you hear the story, see if you have an idea of the place where Paul started the church in Philippi.

The Story

After Paul and Barnabas left Antioch, they went to many cities and told people about Jesus and encouraged them to get together as churches. After they finished their first trip they went back and told the members of the church in Antioch all that they had done. When they were ready to begin another trip, Paul and Barnabas decided to separate into two teams. Paul chose Silas to be his partner and Barnabas chose John Mark. Paul and Silas went to several cities and told the people about Jesus.

One night Paul had a vision from God in which someone was begging him saying: *"Come to Macedonia and help us."* Paul and Silas obeyed God and went to a city in the province of Macedonia that was called Philippi. After they had been there several days, they went outside the city gate to a place by the river. They had heard that some people got together there to pray. One of the people who was there was Lydia who sold expensive purple cloth. She worshipped God. When she heard Paul talk, she was willing to receive Jesus in her heart. She then invited Paul and Silas to her house so that they could tell her family about Jesus. When her family

134

heard, they also decided to believe in Jesus and were baptized.

One day when Paul and Silas were going to the place of prayer, they met a slave girl who had an evil spirit that gave her the power to tell people their future. Her owners made a lot of money because of what she did. This girl kept following Paul and Silas and yelling: *"These men are servants of the Most High God."* After she had done this for several days, Paul said to the spirit, *"In the name of Jesus I order you to come out of this girl."* Immediately the spirit left her and she did not have the power she had before.

The owners of this slave girl were very angry with Paul and Silas and a large crowd or people started shouting against Paul and Silas. This uproar caused the official to grab Paul and Silas and order the soldiers to beat them with a whip. After that they were put in jail with chains on their feet. But about midnight Paul and Silas were praying and singing praises to God. All of a sudden there was an earthquake that shook the jail and all the doors were open and the chains fell from the prisoners.

When the jailer heard this he thought the prisoners had escaped to he pulled out his sword to kill himself. Paul and Silas told him, "do not do that, we are all here." When he saw Paul and Silas he was shaking and fell down in front of them. The jailer then took Paul and Silas out of the jail and he asked them: *"What do I need to do to be saved?"* They told him, *"Put your faith in Jesus and you will be saved not only you but also your family."* The jailer then took Paul and Silas to his house where they told the jailer's family about Jesus. When the jailer and his family put their faith in Jesus Paul baptized them.

After that, Paul and Silas went straight to Lydia's house. There they encouraged the followers of Jesus before they left to go to another city. Paul loved the believers in this city so much that later he wrote them a letter that is part of the Bible.

Post-Story Dialog

In addition to selecting some of the questions listed in the pre-story dialog segment, be sensitive to the leadership of

135

the Holy Spirit. Would it be helpful to stress the "person of peace" concept? Is there enough of an animistic influence to focus on the deliverance of the slave girl and God's attitude toward animistic practices? Will it be helpful to point out that the ministry that was started in two homes was the start of the church in Philippi?

Starting Churches in Homes
(Composite story)[195]
(Acts 18:1-10)

Pre-Story Dialog

Last time we heard the story of the way the church was started in Philippi. Today I am going to tell you how Paul told people about Jesus and when they believed he trained them to tell others about Jesus and to teach them the word of God. As you listen to the story see if you can find out where Paul told people about Jesus.

Also listen to find an answer to these questions: 1) Did Paul stop telling people about Jesus because they closed the doors to him in the Jewish place of worship? 2) Did Paul baptize the new believers? 3) Did Paul train the new believers? 4) Did the new believers that Paul trained follow his example? 4) How did Paul support himself when he went to the different cities to start churches?

The Story

After Paul left Philippi he went to several cities telling people about Jesus until he came to the large city of Corinth. When he got there he met Aquila and Priscilla, a Jewish couple who had been forced to leave Rome when the Emperor ordered all of the Jewish people to get out. When Paul met Aquila and Priscilla he found out that they earned their living just like he did. So Paul stayed with them and they worked together making tents.

Every day of worship Paul went to the Jewish place of worship. There he spoke to the Jews and Gentiles who were there and tried to lead them to believe in Jesus. But after two of his fellow workers (Silas and Timothy) came from Macedonia to join him, Paul spent most of his time telling the Jews that Jesus was the Son of God. Instead of believing, the Jews turned against Paul and insulted him. Paul then told them: *"Whatever happens is going to be your fault. I am now going to tell the Gentile people groups about Jesus."*

Because the Jews did not want Paul to speak in their place of worship, Paul moved into the house of Titus, a man who worshiped God. Even Crispus, the leader of the Jewish worship place, and his whole family believed in Jesus. Many of the people in Corinth believed in Jesus and Paul baptized them. After Paul received a vision from God who told him not to be afraid and to keep telling people about Jesus, Paul decided to stay there in Corinth for a year and a half. Paul then said good-bye to the believers in Corinth and went by ship with Priscilla and Aquila until they got to the city of Ephesus. Paul left them there and went to other cities telling people about Jesus.

When Priscilla and Aquila were in Ephesus they met a man named Apollos. This man was a good speaker and knew the Word of God very well. What he knew about Jesus was very good but he did not know all the story of Jesus. After Priscilla and Aquila heard Apollos they invited him to their home and helped him to understand all the story of Jesus. After that Apollos went to many cities and used the Word of God to prove to the Jewish people that Jesus was the Son of God.

After some years went by Aquila and Pricilla returned to Rome and started a church in their home. Many years later when Paul wrote a letter to the believers in the city of Rome he wrote: *"Please give my greetings to Priscilla and Aquila. They were not only willing to serve with me but to give their lives for me. Not only I but many of the churches of the Gentile people groups are very grateful to them. Please give my greetings to the church that meets in their home"* (Rom. 16:5).

This is the story from God's Word of how Paul started a church in a house at Corinth and how the people he trained, Priscilla and Aquila, started a church in their home in the city of Rome.

Post-Story Dialog

Utilize the questions that are useful from the Pre-Story Dialog section. This is an excellent opportunity to emphasize several important concepts related to church planting: 1) People can witness in their work place; 2) Church planters can support themselves through their various vocations; 3) People who are won to the Lord can be trained to witness to others and to start churches; 4) Churches can be started in homes.

How Paul Started Churches
(Composite Story)
(Acts 13, 14, 15, 16, 18)

Pre-Story Dialog

I have told you the stories of how the apostle Paul started many churches in many cities. In this story I am going to tell about the things Paul did to start these churches. I am going to tell you again some parts of the stories I have already told you. The reason for this is that it helps us to think about these things again. As you listen to the story try to find an answer to these questions: 1) What are some things that Paul did that I can do to start churches?; 2) What are some things I need to do differently?

The Story

Everywhere Paul went he looked for people to talk to them about Jesus. You remember I told you the story that when Paul went to Philippi he found Lydia and a group of women by the riverside and told them about Jesus. You remember also that I told you the story of the way Paul talked to the people in the Jewish place of worship when he went to the city of Corinth. Everywhere Paul went he looked for people to talk to them about Jesus.

When Paul found some people he told them the good news that Jesus died for their sins and if they received them in their hearts God would accept them. You remember that when Lydia heard Paul talk about Jesus she decided to believe in Jesus. She invited Paul to her home to tell her family and they also believed in Jesus. You also remember that when the Jailer heard Paul talk about Jesus he felt sorry for his sins and received Jesus. Like Lydia, the Jailer also wanted his family to hear about Jesus. When they heard Paul talk about Jesus they also believed in Jesus.

When people believed in Jesus Paul baptized them and they became part of the church. When Lydia and her family believed in Jesus, Paul baptized them and they, and the other believers, started meeting in her home. You remember that when Paul went to Corinth he told Priscilla and Aquila about Jesus and they received Jesus in their hearts. Also Crispus and his family believed in Jesus. Paul then baptized Priscilla, Aquila, Crispus and his family, and many other believers and they started meeting in the house of Titus Justus. We see in these stories that when people believed in Jesus they were baptized and they became members of the church that was started there.

After Paul baptized those who believed in Jesus and they started gathering together to worship God, Paul tried to find out from God which were the leaders he had called to guide the church. In the story of how Paul and Barnabas started the church in Lystra you will remember that we said that Paul and Barnabas went back to visit them. When they were there Paul and Barnabas chose leaders for the church. After that they spent a lot of time praying that God would guide them and take care of them. Paul and Barnabas then left the church in the hands of the leaders that were chosen and Paul and Barnabas went to other cities to tell people about Jesus.

Post-Story Dialog

As we have once again looked at the stories of the churches that Paul started, we can learn what he did and what we need to do to start many churches. Be sure and emphasize the very natural way in which Paul planted churches: 1) He looked for people to tell them about Jesus; 2) When Paul found the people he told them about Jesus; 3) When the people believed Paul baptized them; 4) Paul then gathered the people into churches to worship God; 5) Paul then appointed leaders to lead the church. Even though this is a list, it can be told in a story fashion so new believers can have an idea of what they need to do to gather themselves into churches and have the vision to start other congregations.

In this segment we have selected some the stories from the book of Acts that can be utilized for the purpose of training and encouraging believers to start churches. Even though the list of stories is somewhat extensive we want to emphasize that we are not recommending that all of the stories be used at once. The church planting storyer will need to study the worldview of the people group and select the Bible stories that fit best and help the most to encourage the new believers to get involved in church planting. The church planting storyer may want to use a two-tiered approach telling the stories that are most appropriate first and then telling the others to strengthen the church planting later.

Church planting storyers will want to remember that they can begin laying the foundation for church planting from the very beginning of the Evangelism Track so that church planting becomes a part of a very natural process. We also want to remind the storyers that the worldview of the people group will need to be taken into account in the Pre-Story sessions and the Post-Story sessions as well as the selection of the stories themselves. It will also be helpful for the storyer to be aware of the fact that the stories we have included above are primarily paraphrased stories. The storyer may need to adapt the terminology and the presentation of the story to the ministry focus group.

Stories to Strengthen Churches

The stories we have shared above related to church starting. In this section we are going to suggest stories that can be used to strengthen the churches that have been started. It will be helpful for the church planter to have a repertoire of stories that can be used to address specific issues that need to be dealt with. Due to the fact that many of these stories can already be found in the Discipleship Track and that these need to be used only as a situation arises, we are not going to develop these stories but merely to suggest the issues and the stories that can be used to address them.

Issue: Dishonesty in the Church

Story: Ananias and Sapphira (Acts)

Issue: Discrimination in the church

Story: The Grecian Widows (Acts 6)

Peter and Cornelius (Acts10)

Issue: Persecution

Story: Peter's Deliverance (Acts 12)

Story: Review story of Stephen's Martyrdom (Acts 7)

Issue: Imposing Unbiblical Standards

Story: Jerusalem Council (Acts 15)

Issue: Idolatry/Animism

Story: Paul at Athens (Acts 17)

Story: Simon the Sorcerer (story within a story) (Acts 8)

Story: Power Encounter with Elymas (Acts 13:4-12)

Issue: How to Give Your Testimony

Story: Paul's Testimony (Acts 22)

Issue: Divine Intervention

Story: Paul's Deliverance from Shipwreck (Acts 27)

Additional resources for storying that undergird church planting efforts can be found in the *Following Jesus: Living in the Family of Jesus series.*[196] Discs 5, 6 and 7 deal with such topics as:

- Early Church-Barnabas, Annanias and Sapphira
- Choosing Seven Helpers at the Church in Jerusalem
- Church Faces Persecution – Stephen Martyred
- Saul's Conversion
- Lord's Supper (A Church Remembers Her Savior)
- Peter and Cornelius (A Church Sees Beyond Itself to the Lost Among Other People Groups)
- Jerusalem and Antioch Churches Cooperate.
- Calling out the first missionaries at Antioch
- The Jerusalem Council
- A church pastor's responsibility
- Leaders in the church

- Spiritual gifts and the body of Christ
- Where churches meet
- The purpose of the church.[197]

The presenters of the *Following Jesus Series* utilize a storying format to communicate to the trainees the biblical concepts of the nature and function or a church. The trainees will in turn be able to take these Bible stories and teach new converts in a people group what a church is and how they can gather themselves into groups that carry out the functions and ministries of a church. This excellent resource can save storying church planters a great deal of time and effort. They can listen to these stories, decide which ones are needed in their setting, and adapt their presentation to their people group.

Church Planting Movement Storying
Written by LaNette Thompson

In addition to these church planting story sets that we have shared above, we want to include a valuable resource that LaNette Thompson has developed. Concerned that some Bible storyers were not being intentional enough about starting churches among their people groups, in 2003 LaNette decided to work on a Church Planting Storying Track that she could share with the storyers in her area. Even though her multiple responsibilities have prevented her from including more stories in this track, what she has developed is very helpful and insightful.

She has highlighted a list of truths from the story that need to be emphasized, key questions that need to be asked in the storying sessions, and concepts from the Church Planting Movements approach that need to be considered. These truths, questions, and concepts will make it possible for the storyer to be better informed and more focused on the goals that must be kept in mind while sharing Bible stories with a specific people group. She has graciously agreed to contribute this Church Planting Movement Storying Track to this chapter.

These stories can greatly strengthen church planting efforts in many parts of the world. The questions she has framed and the "truths from the story" she has highlighted can provide excellent material for the stories we have shared above as well as other stories that are developed and used in church planting efforts. With gratitude we include her storying track in this segment of this chapter.

The First Church Is Planted
Text: Acts 1:10-26; Acts 2

The listeners will discover the following truths and concepts during the discussion time following the story. They are not to be "taught" or "listed" prior to or during the discussion time.

Truths from the story:

- The disciples devoted themselves to prayer.

- They were committed to following God's plan.

- They waited on the Holy Spirit and when he came, allowed themselves to be led by him.

- The believers were baptized immediately upon repenting and accepting Christ.

- Following their baptism, the believers all participated in the work of the church by teaching, sharing their possessions, worshiping, and eating together.

- They met at the temple as well as in small groups in their homes.

- There was no paid leadership.

- They lived in an attitude of praise and thanksgiving.

- Unbelievers noticed something different about them and liked what they saw.

- It was the Lord who added to their number those who were being saved.

The following are 10 elements seen in Church Planting Movements. [198] As we go through these, one-

143

by-one, tell us how they relate or do not relate to this biblical story.

From 10 Universal Elements: [199]

1. Importance of prayer.

2. Abundant gospel sowing.

3. Intentional church planting

4. Scriptural authority (in this case apostolic).

5. Local leadership.

6. Lay leadership.

7. Cell or house churches.

8. Churches planting churches.

9. Rapid reproduction.

10. Healthy churches comprising 1) worship, 2) evangelistic and missionary outreach, 3) education and discipleship, 4) ministry, and 5) fellowship.

The following are 10 factors in a Church Planting Movement. As we go through them one-by-one, tell how each relates or does not relate to this biblical story.

From 10 Factors[200]

1. Worship in the heart language.

2. Evangelism has communal implications.

3. Rapid incorporation of new converts into the life and ministry of the church.

4. Passion and fearlessness.

5. A price to pay to become a Christian.

6. Perceived leadership crisis or spiritual vacuum in society.

7. On-the-job training for church leadership.

8. Leadership authority is decentralized.

9. Outsiders keep a low profile.

10. Missionaries suffer.

The following are POUCH principles. As we go through them one-by-one, tell how each relates or does not relate to this biblical story.

From POUCH (Participative, Obedience to Scripture, Unpaid leadership, Cell and House churches)[201]

1. Participative Bible study and worship groups.

2. Obedience to the Bible. Believers are responsible for immediately putting into practice any truth they learn from Scripture or through the Holy Spirit.

3. Unpaid and non-hierarchical leadership.

4. Cell groups/house churches.

The following are MAWL principles. As we go through them one-by-one, tell how each relates or does not relate to this biblical story.

From MAWL (Model, Assist, Watch, and Leave)[202]

1. Missionaries model biblical teaching and lifestyle.

2. Missionaries assist new leadership. More than one leader in a group.

3. Missionaries watch, leaving them on their own, then returning to strengthen and encourage as necessary.

4. Missionaries leave.

The following are common obstacles to Church Planting Movements. As we go through them one-by-one, discuss which obstacles you feel are occurring in your area that are keeping you from experiencing a CPM.

From Obstacles to CPMs[203]

1. Imposing extra-biblical requirements for being a church.

2. Loss of valued cultural identity.

3. Overcoming bad examples of Christianity.

4. Non-reproducible church models.

145

5. Subsidies creating dependency.

6. Extra-biblical leadership requirements.

7. Linear, sequential thought and practice.

8. Planting "frog" rather than "lizard" churches.

9. Prescriptive strategies.

Story

The disciples had watched, astonished as Jesus ascended into heaven. Two men, dressed in white, asked them, "Why do you stand here looking into the sky? *This same Jesus, who has been taken from you into heaven, will come back in the same way you have seen him go into heaven."*

So, the disciples returned to Jerusalem, as they were a day's walk from the city at the Mount of Olives. When they arrived, they went upstairs to the room where they were staying. There were the disciples, Peter and John, James and Andrew, Philip and Thomas, Bartholomew and Matthew, James son of Alpheus and Simon the Zealot, and Judas son of James. Jesus' brothers were also there along with his mother Mary and some other women. They all joined together constantly in prayer. There were about 120 of them. One man, Matthias, who had been with them from the beginning of Jesus' ministry, was chosen to be an apostle and to fill Judas Iscariot's place. After Judas had betrayed Jesus, Judas had bought a field and it was in that field that he had died.

Many weeks went by. Then, one day, when they were all together in a house the day of Pentecost came. Suddenly a sound like the blowing of a violent wind came from heaven and filled the whole house. They saw what seemed to be tongues of fire that separated and came to rest on each of them. All of them were filled with the Holy Spirit and began to speak in other languages as the Spirit guided them.

Now, there were devout Jews from every nation in the world living in Jerusalem. When they heard the sounds of Pentecost, a great crowd gathered. The people were astonished because each one heard his language being spoken by the disciples. They asked, *"Aren't these people from Galilee? How is it that we hear, each of us in our own* mother tongue? We hear them telling in our own languages about the mighty works of God." They were amazed and asked each other, "What does this mean?"

But others made fun of the disciples and said, "They are drunk!"

But Peter, standing with the other eleven apostles, spoke loudly, saying, "Men of Judea and all who live in Jerusalem listen to me. These men are not drunk as you are saying. It is only 9:00 a.m.! But this is what was told about by the prophet Joel, 'And in the last days it shall be, God declares, that I will pour out my Spirit upon all people and your sons and your daughters shall prophesy and your young men shall see visions and your old men shall dream dreams...And I will show wondrous things in the heaven above and signs on the earth beneath, blood, and fire, and vapor of smoke; the sun shall be turned into darkness and the moon into blood, before the day of the Lord comes. And it shall be that whoever calls on the name of the Lord shall be saved.'

Peter cried, "Men of Israel, hear these words: Jesus of Nazareth, a man shown worthy to you by God with mighty works and miracles which God did through him in your midst, this Jesus, delivered up according to God's definite plan and knowledge, this Jesus, you crucified and killed. But God raised him up, freeing him from the agony of death, because it was not possible for death to hold him.

For David said about him: "I saw the Lord always before me, for he is at my right hand that I may not be shaken. Therefore, my heart is glad and my tongue rejoices. My body will live in hope because you will not abandon me to the grave..."

"Brothers," Peter continued, "I can tell you confidently that the patriarch David both died and was buried and his tomb is with us to this day. Being a prophet and knowing that God had sworn with an oath to him that he would set one of his descendants upon his throne, he foresaw and spoke of the resurrection of the Christ. This Jesus, God raised up, and of that we are all witnesses. Exalted to the right hand of God and having received from the Father the promise of the Holy Spirit, he has poured out this which you see and hear...Let all the people of Israel know for certain *that God has made him both Lord and Christ, this Jesus whom you crucified."*

When the people heard this, they were cut to the heart and said to Peter and the rest of the disciples, *"Brothers, what shall we do?"*

And Peter said to them, *"Repent and be baptized every one of you in the name of Jesus Christ for the forgiveness of your sins, and you will receive the gift of the Holy Spirit. The promise is for you and your children and for all who are far off—everyone whom the Lord our God calls to him."*

With many other words Peter warned them saying: *"Save yourselves from this corrupt generation."* Those who accepted his message were baptized. About 3,000 people were added to their number that day. And they devoted themselves to the apostles' teaching and to fellowship, to the breaking of bread and to prayer.

Everyone was filled with wonder and the apostles did many miracles. All the believers were together and shared with each other. Selling their possessions and goods, they gave to anyone as he had need. Every day they continued to meet together at the temple and in their homes. They ate together in their homes with joyful and sincere hearts, praising God. And all the other people approved of them.

And the Lord added to their number day by day, those who were being saved.

Questions:

- What did the disciples do as they met together following Jesus' ascension into heaven? (Pray.)

- About how many believers were there at that time? (About 120.)

- Why do you think they prayed instead of going about the city telling others what they had seen? (They did not have the Holy Spirit. Jesus had told them earlier to watch and pray. They wanted to follow God's plan.)

- What does this teach us about the importance of prayer?

- What does this teach us about the importance of waiting on God?

- Describe what happened on the day of Pentecost.

- When the Holy Spirit came upon the disciples, did they stay in their room enjoying the power the Spirit gave them? (No.) Why not? (Others had heard the sound and came to investigate.)

- What was significant about the disciples speaking in different languages and the people from different nations hearing in their own language about the mighty works of God? (It showed that the message was for all peoples. It foretold what was to come.)

- What happened when the people were touched by Peter's message and accepted the gospel? (They were baptized.)

- Why do you think they were baptized immediately? (There was nothing stopping them from being baptized.)

- How many people were added to their number that day? (About 3,000.)

- Who do you think baptized these people? (No information is given in Scripture. If only the apostles did that would mean each apostle had to baptize 250 people.)

- Who authorized these people to be baptized? (No information is given in Scripture.)

- If Pentecost had occurred in your area today, would the people have been able to be baptized immediately? Why or why not?

- What are some of the benefits of immediate baptism? What are some of the difficulties in immediate baptism?

- How did the believers live out their faith? (By sharing their possessions and fellowshipping together.)

- How do believers in your area live out their faith?

- On the whole, who takes better care of the needy in their care, the Muslims or the Christians? Why or why not?

- How well do the believers in your area do about taking care of the needy in their churches? Why or why not?

- How did the people in the community at the time of Pentecost feel about the believers? (They approved of them.)

- Why do you think the people in the community approved of the believers? (Because of their lifestyle.)

- How do the people in your area feel about the believers in your church? Why do they feel this way?

- Where did the believers meet? (In the temple and in homes.)

- Where do the people in your area meet?

- What are the difficulties in meeting only in a church building? What are the benefits?

- What are the difficulties in meeting in homes? What are the benefits?

- Do all of the people in your congregation know where everyone else lives?

- If you are the pastor, do you know where all of your members live?

- What are the requirements in your area for someone to be a pastor?

- If those requirements had been applied to the apostles, would they be allowed to be a pastor in your area?

- What do you think would happen in your community if the believers in your church began acting in the same way as the believers following Pentecost, living in joy and constant praise for God's goodness?

- What was the apostles' plan for evangelism? (There is no information about a plan. They just lived out their faith each day.)
- Who added to their number those who were being saved? (The Lord.)[204]

The Church as a Seedling
Text: Acts 3; Acts 4

The listeners will discover the following truths and concepts during the discussion time following the story. They are not to be "taught" or "listed" prior to or during the discussion time.

Truths from the story:

- The disciples devoted themselves to prayer.
- They were ordinary, uneducated men but men who had had an experience with Jesus.
- They were committed to following God's plan.
- They were filled with the Holy Spirit.
- They preached Jesus.
- They were willing to risk persecution.
- In times of trouble, the believers praised God and prayed for boldness.
- The believers showed love to each other and took care of their own.

CPM Concepts205: How many of these relate or do not relate to this biblical story?

- *From 10 Universal Elements*: 1, 2, 4, 5. 6. 7. 10. (See list in 1st Story)
- *From 10 Common Factors:* 1. 2. 3. 4. (See list in 1st Story)
- From POUCH": *1. 2. 3. 4. (See list in 1st Story)*

Story

One day, the apostles Peter and John were going to the temple at the time of prayer at three in the afternoon, when a man who had been crippled from birth was being carried to the temple gate to beg for money. When the man saw Peter and John about to enter the temple courtyard, he asked for money. Peter and John looked straight at him. Then Peter said, *"Look at us!"* So, expecting to get some money, the man lifted up his eyes. But Peter said, *"I have no silver and gold, but I give you what I have; in the name of Jesus Christ of Nazareth, walk."*

And taking him by the right hand, he helped the beggar up. Instantly, the man's feet and ankles became strong. He jumped to his feet and began to walk. Then he entered the temple with them, walking and leaping and praising God. When all the people saw him walking and praising God, they knew he was the beggar who used to sit every day by the temple gate, and they were filled with wonder and amazement at what had happened to him.

While the beggar held on to Peter and John, all the people came running to them in the place called Solomon's Colonnade. When Peter saw this, he said to them, *"Men of Israel, why does this surprise you? Why are you staring at us as if by our own power or godliness we had made this man walk? The God of Abraham, Isaac and Jacob, the God of our fathers, has glorified his servant Jesus, whom you denied and handed over to Pilate to be killed. You denied the Holy and Righteous One, and asked for a murderer to be released to you. You killed the author of life, but God raised him from the dead. We are witnesses of this. And his name and the faith which is through Jesus have given the man this perfect health in the presence of you all."*

"Now, brothers, I know that you acted in ignorance, as did your leaders. But this is how God fulfilled what he had foretold through all the prophets, saying that his Christ would suffer. Repent, then, and turn to God so that your sins may be wiped out, that times of refreshing may come from the Lord, and that he may send the Christ, who has been appointed for you—even Jesus. He must remain in heaven

until the time comes for God to restore everything, as he promised long ago through his holy prophets.

For Moses said, 'The Lord your God will raise up for you a prophet like me from among your own people; you must listen to everything he tells you. Anyone who does not listen to him will be completely cut off from among his people.'"

"Indeed, all the prophets from Samuel on have foretold these days. You are the children of these prophets and of the covenant that God made with your fathers. God said to Abraham, 'Through your offspring all peoples on earth will be blessed.' When God raised up his servant, he sent him first to you to bless you in turning every one of you from your wickedness."

While they were speaking, the priests and the captain of the temple guard and the Sadducees came up to them. The Sadducees were very disturbed because the apostles were teaching the people and proclaiming in Jesus the resurrection of the dead. They arrested them and put them in jail until the next day as it was already evening.

But many who heard the message believed, and the number of believers who were men grew to about five thousand.

The next day the rulers, elders, and teachers of the law met in Jerusalem. They had Peter and John brought before them and asked them, "By what power or what name did you do this?"

Then Peter, filled with the Holy Spirit, said to them: *"If you are asking us about this act of kindness we showed to a cripple and are asking how he was healed then you and all the people of Israel must know that it is by the name of Jesus Christ of Nazareth whom you crucified but whom God raised from the dead that this man stands before you healed. Salvation is found in no one else, for there is no other name under heaven given to men by which we must be saved."*

When the temple leaders saw Peter and John's courage and realized that they were uneducated, ordinary men, they were astonished and they recognized that these men had been with Jesus. But since they could see the man who had been healed standing there with them, there was nothing they could say. They ordered them out of the room and talked together. *"Everybody living in Jerusalem knows they have done an outstanding miracle, and we cannot deny it. But to stop this thing from spreading any further among the people, we must warn these men to speak no longer to anyone in this name."*

So they called them in again and ordered them not to speak or teach at all in the name of Jesus. But Peter and John replied, *"You decide whether we should obey you or God, for we can't help speaking about what we have seen and heard.*

After further threats, the religious leaders let them go because they couldn't decide how to punish them because all the people were praising God for the healing of the beggar who had been lame for over forty years.

When they were released, Peter and John went back to the believers and reported all that had happened. When the people heard this, they raised their voices together in prayer, praising God and asking him to help them speak his word with boldness in spite of the threats. *"Stretch out your hand to heal and perform miraculous signs and wonders through the name of your holy servant Jesus,"* they prayed. After they prayed, the place where they were meeting was shaken. And they were all filled with the Holy Spirit and spoke the word of God boldly.

All the believers were united in heart and mind. They shared everything they had. The apostles continued to testify to the resurrection of the Lord Jesus with great power, and much grace was upon them. There were no needy persons among the believers for from time to time, those who owned lands or houses sold them, brought the money from the sales and put it at the apostles' feet to be distributed to anyone in need. In this same fashion, a Levite named Joseph whom the apostles called Barnabas which means Son of Encouragement, sold a field he owned and gave the money to the apostles.

Questions:

- Why were Peter and John going to the temple? (It was the time of prayer.)

- Why do you think Peter and John did not give the beggar any money? (They didn't have any.)

- Who gave Peter the power to heal this man? (The Holy Spirit through the name of Jesus.)

- Was the beggar expecting to be healed? (No.)

- What was it that healed the man? (Faith in the name of Jesus.)

- Do you think Peter and John had planned to preach to the crowds that day? (Probably not.)

- Why did they begin preaching? (The crowds had gathered. The Holy Spirit led them.)

- Why were the authorities upset? (Because in talking about Jesus they were talking about the resurrection of the dead.)

- What happened to Peter and John? (They were put in prison.)

- Do you think the religious leaders were meeting the spiritual needs of the people who were coming to the temple? Did they appear to care about the questions the people were asking?

- What were the results of Peter and John's preaching? (The number of men grew to about 5,000.)

- Did Peter preach before the religious rulers in his own power? (No.) In whose power? (The Holy Spirit.)

- Why were the religious rulers surprised? (Because Peter and John were ordinary uneducated men.)

- Even though Peter and John were ordinary, uneducated men, what made the difference? (They had been with Jesus.)

- Is it possible for an ordinary, uneducated man to "be with Jesus" today?

- Does an education help us to know God better?

- What are the benefits of having an education? What are the drawbacks of having an education?

- What instructions did the religious leaders give Peter and John? (Not to preach in Jesus' name.)

- How did Peter and John respond? (They asked if it were better to obey God or the religious rulers.)

- Do you think Peter and John were afraid? Why or why not?

- Why did the threat of persecution not stop Peter and John from preaching? (They were following God's plan.)

- Where did Peter and John go when they were released? (Back to their own people, the believers.)

- What did the believers do immediately when Peter and John told them about the religious leaders' threats? (They called out to God in prayer.)

- What did they pray for? (Boldness and more miracles.)

- What happened after they prayed? (The place where they were meeting was shaken and they were all filled with the Holy Spirit and spoke the word of God boldly.)

- Why was there no needy person among the believers? (From time to time, people sold things that belonged to them in order to share with others.)

- Who decided when something had to be sold? (No one.) Why did they do it? (Out of love.)

The Church Reproduces and is Pruned
Text: Acts 11:19-30; 12:24-25; 13:1-5, 46-52; 14:21-28; Acts 15:1-35

The listeners will discover the following truths and concepts during the discussion time following the story. They are not to be "taught" or "listed" prior to or during the discussion time.

Truths from the Story:

- Believers shared the gospel wherever they went.
- New churches were formed when people shared and people believed.
- Mature believers taught and encouraged the new churches.
- The new church became financially independent and reached out to help other believers in need.
- The new church spent time in prayer, fasting, and listening to God's Word.
- There was more than one leader in the churches.
- The Holy Spirit urged the new church to send out its own teachers to begin other churches.
- The new church was obedient to the Holy Spirit and sent out missionaries.
- The missionaries preached the gospel, endured hardships, began churches, taught, and moved on, leaving the churches in the hands of local leadership.
- The apostles and elders did not want to make it difficult for those from other ethnic groups to turn to God.
- Under the direction of the Holy Spirit, the apostles and elders examined their own tradition and laws and changed their requirements in order to free the new believers from the burden of the law.

CPM Concepts: How many of these relate or do not relate to this biblical story?

- From 10 Universal Elements: 1. 2. 3. 4. 5. 6. 7. 8. 10.
- From 10 Common Factors: 1. 2. 3. 4, 5. 6. 7. 8. 9. 10
- From POUCH: 1.2.3.4.
- From MAWL: 1. 2. 3. 4.
- From Obstacles to CPMs: 1. 2. 3. 4. 5. 6. 7. 8. 9.

157

Story

Now those who had been scattered by the persecution following the murder of Stephen, traveled as far as Phoenicia, Cyprus and Antioch, telling the gospel message only to Jews. Some of them, however, men from Cyprus and Cyrene, went to Antioch and began to speak to Greeks also, telling them the good news about the Lord Jesus. A great number that believed turned to the Lord.

News of this reached the church at Jerusalem, and they sent Barnabas to Antioch. When he arrived and saw the evidence of the grace of God, he was glad and encouraged them all to remain true to the Lord with all their hearts. Barnabas was a good man, full of the Holy Spirit and faith, and a great number of people were brought to the Lord.

Then Barnabas went to Tarsus to look for Saul, and when he found him, he brought him to Antioch. So for a whole year, Barnabas and Saul met with the church and taught great numbers of people. Antioch was the first place the disciples were called Christians.

During this time, a prophet from Jerusalem came to Antioch and predicted that a severe famine would spread over the entire Roman world. The disciples, each according to his ability, decided to provide help for the brothers living in Judea. They sent Barnabas and Saul to take their gift to the elders in Jerusalem. When they had finished their mission, Barnabas and Saul returned to Antioch taking a young man, John Mark, with them.

In the church there were prophets and teachers: Barnabas, Simeon called Niger, Lucius of Cyrene, Manaen (who had been brought up with Herod the tetrarch) and Saul. While they were worshiping the Lord and fasting, the Holy Spirit said, *"Set apart for me Barnabas and Saul for the work to which I have called them."* So after they had fasted and prayed, they placed their hands on them and sent them off.

The two of them, sent on their way by the Holy Spirit, went down to Seleucia and sailed from there to Cyprus. When they arrived at Salamis, they proclaimed the word of God in the Jewish synagogues. John Mark was with them as their helper. They traveled and preached and the word of the Lord spread through the whole region. They encountered hardships and persecution, mostly from the Jews. Paul and Barnabas told them, "We had to speak the word of God to you first. Since you reject it and do not consider yourselves worthy of eternal life, we now turn to the Gentiles. For this is what the Lord has commanded us: 'I have made you a light for the Gentiles, that you may bring salvation to the ends of the earth.'

When the Gentiles heard this, they were glad and honored the word of the Lord; and all who were appointed for eternal life believed. When Saul, now called Paul, and Barnabas were expelled from a region for preaching the good news, they shook the dust from their feet in protest against them and went to other places. Often they returned to the churches that had begun, strengthening the disciples and encouraging them to remain true to the faith. *"We must go through many hardships to enter the kingdom of God,"* they said. Paul and Barnabas appointed elders for them in each church, and with prayer and fasting, committed them to the Lord, in whom they had put their trust.

After some time, they sailed back to Antioch where they had been committed to the grace of God for the work they had now completed. On arriving there, they gathered the church together and reported all that God had done through them and how he had opened the door of faith to the Gentiles. And they stayed there a long time with the disciples.

Some men came down from Judea to Antioch and were teaching the brothers that unless they were circumcised according to the custom taught by Moses that they could not be saved. This brought Paul and Barnabas in sharp dispute and debate with them. So Paul and Barnabas and some other believers were appointed to go to Jerusalem to see the apostles and elders about this question. The church sent them on their way. As they traveled, they shared the news about the conversion of many Gentiles. The church in Jerusalem, to whom they reported everything God had done through them, welcomed them.

Some believers who were also Pharisees said that the Gentiles must be circumcised and required to obey the Law of Moses. The apostles and elders met to consider this question. After much discussion, Peter got up and addressed them, *"Brothers, you know that some time ago God made a choice among you that the Gentiles might hear from my lips the message of the gospel and believe. God, who knows the heart, showed that he accepted them by giving the Holy Spirit to them, just as he did to us. He made no distinction between us and them, for he cleansed their hearts by faith. Now then, why do you try to test God by putting on the necks of the disciples a yoke that neither we nor our fathers have been able to bear? No! We believe it is through the grace of our Lord Jesus that we are saved, just as they are."*

The whole assembly became silent as they listened to Barnabas and Paul telling about the miracles God had done among the Gentiles from them. When they finished, James quoted the prophets who said that the Gentiles would seek the Lord. He said, *"It is my judgment, therefore, that we should not make it difficult for the Gentiles who are turning to God. Instead we should write to them, telling them to abstain from food polluted by idols, from sexual immorality, from the meat of strangled animals and from blood."*

Then the apostles and elders, with the whole church, decided to choose some of their own men and send them to Antioch with Paul and Barnabas. With them they sent a letter saying that they had heard that some had gone out from them, disturbing the believers by what they said and they were sending Judas (called Barsabbas) and Silas to confirm by word of mouth what they were writing. The letter continued, *"It seemed good to the Holy Spirit and to us not to burden you with anything beyond the following requirements: You are to abstain from food sacrificed to idols, from blood, from the meat of strangled animals and from sexual immorality. You will do well to avoid these things."*

The men were sent off to Antioch where they gathered the church together and delivered the letter. The people read it and were glad for its encouraging message. Judas and Silas, who themselves were prophets, said much to encourage and strengthen the brothers. After spending some time there, they were sent off by the brothers with the blessing of peace to return to those who had sent them. But Paul and Barnabas remained in Antioch, where they and many others taught and preached the word of the Lord.

Questions

- What did the believers do when they were scattered because of the persecution? (They shared the gospel message wherever they went.)

- Do you think our believers today share the gospel message wherever they go? Why or why not?

- What happened when new people accepted Christ? (They formed a church. We know this because the Scripture says Barnabas met with the church at Antioch.)

- Who gave them the authority to form a church? (The Holy Spirit.)

- Why do you think there was a need for a lot of teaching in the church? (The Gentiles did not all know the stories of the Old Testament which are a foundation for New Testament truths.)

- Why do you think Barnabas went to search for Saul? (Perhaps the Holy Spirit urged him.)

- Who do you think was more educated, Barnabas or Saul? (Saul.)

- If Saul had more education, shouldn't he be the one teaching Barnabas? Why or why not?

- How do we know that the new church was financially independent from the Jerusalem church? (They took an offering and sent it back to the Jerusalem church.)

- Who told the Antioch church they had to cooperate with the Jerusalem church and help support it? (No one.) Why did they send the offering? (They did it out of love.)

- How did the church spend its time? (Prayer, fasting, teaching, and reaching out to those in need.)

- How does your church spend its time?

- How many teachers and leaders were there in the church? (Several.)

- Who told the church to set aside Barnabas and Saul? (The Holy Spirit.)

- What was the church doing when the Holy Spirit spoke to them? (Praying and fasting.)

- What does this tell us about the importance of prayer in the Antioch church?

- During the prayer time at your church, do your people mostly talk to God or listen?

- If God were to tell your church people to do something, how would they react?

- How did the Antioch church respond to the Holy Spirit's urging? (They obeyed.)

- If some people in your church felt the Holy Spirit was telling them to send out missionaries to another people group, what procedure would the church have to go through to follow through? How long would that take?

- What made it easier for the Antioch church to send away two of their teachers? (They had other leaders and teachers in the church.)

- What does this teach us about the importance of having multiple leaders in our churches?

- Did Barnabas and Saul continue the principle of training leaders? (Yes.) How do we know? (They took John Mark with them.)

- How many teachers and leaders are in your churches?

- What are the advantages of having multiple teachers and leaders in our churches? What are the disadvantages?

- What kind of life did Barnabas and Saul lead during their missionary journey? (They taught and began churches. They experienced hardships, persecution, and suffering.)

- Who supported them? (They worked.)

- When they began a church, did Barnabas and Saul send word to Antioch so they could send a pastor to lead the church? (No.) Why not?

- Who led the churches Barnabas and Saul began?

- Did Barnabas and Saul decide to move and stay with the churches they began? (No.) Why not? (They had other work to do.)

- What is the difference between the role of a missionary and the role of a pastor? (A missionary starts new work and a pastor continues and grows the work.)

- What did Barnabas and Saul do when they returned to Antioch? (Called the church together and reported on what they had done.)

- When some teachers from Jerusalem came to Antioch, why did their teaching cause problems? (They were teaching that the Gentiles must be circumcised in order to be saved.)

- How did the church respond? (They sent Barnabas and Saul to Jerusalem to discuss the matter.)

- Why did James feel the Gentiles did not have to be circumcised? (Because it would make it difficult for them to turn to God.)

- Why is the Council at Jerusalem and their advice to the Gentile believers important in the life of the church? (It underscored salvation by grace and not works or the law.)

- What are some things that we as Christians do that might make it difficult for people to turn to God?

- What does it mean to "become a Christian" in the eyes of the world?

- Why is it difficult for a Muslim to "become a Christian?"

- What do you think would have happened if the Jerusalem Council said the Gentile believers must be circumcised in order to be saved?

- Are there laws or traditions in our churches that we need to re-examine that might be stumbling blocks to others hearing about or coming to Christ?

The Church Bears Fruit
Text: Acts 15:36-41; 16:1-40

The listeners will discover the following truths and concepts during the discussion time following the story. They are not to be "taught" or "listed" prior to or during the discussion time.

Truths from the story:

- Missionaries and teachers used the apprentice method to train new leaders.

- Prayer is a vital part of ministry.

- The Holy Spirit directs us where we are to begin new work.

- The church can meet anywhere, by a river, in a house, or in a building.

- New believers were baptized immediately.

- Missionaries often suffer for the sake of the gospel.

- Paul was self-supporting during his missionary journeys.

CPM Concepts: How many of these relate or do not relate to this biblical story?

- *From 10 Universal Elements: 1. 2. 3. 4. 5. 6. 7. 9. 10.*

- *From 10 Common Factors: 1. 2. 3. 4. 5. 6. 7. 8. 9. 10.*

- *From POUCH: 1. 2. 3. 4.*

- *From MAWL (Model, Assist, Watch, and Leave): 1. 2. 3. 4.*

Story

Some time after Paul and Barnabas had been in Antioch, Paul said to Barnabas, "*Let us go back and visit the believers in all the towns where we preached the word of the Lord and see how they are doing.*" Barnabas wanted to take John Mark with them, but Paul did not think it was wise to take him because he had not continued with them in the work but left them during their journey.

They had such a sharp disagreement that they parted ways, Barnabas taking John Mark and Paul choosing Silas. They went to different areas, strengthening the churches. Paul went to Derbe where a young disciple named Timothy lived. His mother was a Jewess and a believer, but his father was a Greek. Paul wanted to take him along on the journey, so he circumcised him so as not to offend the Jews in that area.

As they traveled from town to town, they delivered the decisions reached by the apostles and elders in Jerusalem for the people to obey. So the churches were strengthened in the faith and grew daily in numbers.

Paul and his companions traveled throughout the region of Phrygia and Galatia, having been kept by the Holy Spirit from preaching the word in the province of Asia. In one area that they tried to enter, the Spirit would not allow them, so they went to another place. There, during the night, Paul had a vision of a man of Macedonia standing and begging him, "*Come over to Macedonia and help us.*" Following the vision, he and his companions left for Macedonia, concluding that God had called them to preach the gospel to them.

When they arrived in the area, they went outside a city gate to a river, expecting to find a place of prayer. They encountered a woman named Lydia, who was a worshiper of God. The Lord opened her heart to Paul's message. When she and the members of her household were baptized, she invited Paul and his companions to stay at her house.

Once, Paul and Silas prayed for a slave girl who had a spirit by which she predicted the future. When the spirit left her in response to their prayer, her owners were furious because they realized they wouldn't make any more money from her predictions. They stirred up a crowd and lied about Paul and Silas to the authorities. As a result, Paul and Silas were stripped and severely beaten, then thrown into prison. The jailer was commanded to guard them carefully, so he put them in chains in an inner cell.

About midnight, Paul and Silas were praying and singing hymns to God, and the other prisoners were listening to them. Suddenly, there was such a violent earthquake, that the foundations of the prison were shaken. At once all the prison doors flew open, and everybody's chains came loose. The jailer woke up, and when he saw the prison doors open, he drew his sword and was about to kill himself because he thought the prisoners had escaped. But Paul shouted, *"Don't harm yourself! We are all here!"*

The jailer called for lights, rushed in and fell trembling before Paul and Silas. He then brought them out and asked, *"Sirs, what must I do to be saved?"*

They replied, *"Believe in the Lord Jesus, and you will be saved—you and your household."* Then they shared God's word with him and with all the others in his house. At that hour of the night the jailer took them and washed their wounds; then immediately he and all his family were baptized. The jailer brought them into his house and set a meal before them; he was filled with joy because he had come to believe in God—he and his whole family.

When it was daylight, the authorities ordered Paul and Silas to be released. The jailer told them they could leave and to go in peace. But Paul said to the officers that they would have to escort them out because they were Roman citizens but had been beaten without a trial and thrown into prison. This disturbed the authorities, as they had not known that they were Roman citizens. They came and apologized to Paul and Silas and asked them to leave the city.

After Paul and Silas came out of prison, they went to Lydia's house, where they met with the believers and encouraged them. Then they left.

Paul and his companions traveled to many different areas, sharing the gospel and starting new churches. They endured many hardships. After some time, when Paul was returning to Jerusalem and was not able to stop by Ephesus, a place where he had begun work, he called for the elders to come to them.

When they arrived he said to them, *"You know how I lived the whole time I was with you, from the first day I came into the province of Asia. I served the Lord with great humanity and with tears, although I was severely tested by the plots of the Jews. You know that I have not hesitated to preach anything that would be helpful to you but have taught you publicly and from house to house...the Holy Spirit warns me that prison and hardships are facing me. However, I consider my life worth nothing to me, if only I may finish the race and complete the task the Lord Jesus has given me—the task of testifying to the gospel of God's grace....Keep watch over yourselves and all the flock of which the Holy Spirit has made you overseers. Be shepherds of the church of God, which he bought with his own blood. I know that after I leave, savage wolves will come in among you and will not spare the flock. Even from your own number men will arise and distort the truth in order to draw away disciples after them. So be on your guard! Remember that for three years I never stopped warning each of you night and day with tears."*

"Now I commit you to God and to the word of his grace, which can build you up and give you an inheritance among all those who are being sanctified. I have not coveted anyone's silver or gold or clothing. You yourselves know that these hands of mine have supplied my own needs and the needs of my companions. In everything I did, I showed you that by this kind of hard work we must help the weak, remembering the words the Lord Jesus himself said, 'It is more blessed to give than to receive.'"

When he had said this, he knelt down with all of them and prayed. They all wept as they embraced him and kissed him. What grieved them most was his statement that they would never see his face again. Then they accompanied him to the ship.

Questions

- Why did Paul and Barnabas separate? (They had a disagreement over taking John Mark.)

- Did Paul go alone? (No.) Who went with him? (Silas.)
- Who else joined their trip? (Timothy.)
- Why do you think Paul wanted Timothy along? (To train him as a leader.)
- From other Scripture that you know, was Paul an effective trainer?
- What does this teach us about the importance of apprenticeship in training leaders?
- How did Paul and Silas know where they were to begin work? (The Holy Spirit told them.)
- How did the Holy Spirit speak to them? (Through prayer and visions.)
- How important should prayer be in the life of a missionary? Why or why not?
- Where did the churches meet? (Anywhere... in the temple courtyards, by the river, in a home.)
- How many church buildings did Paul and Silas build? (None are recorded in Scripture.)
- Why do you think they did not build church buildings?
- How would their ministry have been different if they had practiced church planting as we practice it today?
- When was Lydia and the other believers by the river baptized? (Immediately.)
- Why do you think they were baptized immediately?
- How would you characterize Paul's life?
- If he were doing God's will, why did he endure so much suffering and hardship?
- How was Paul supported during his missionary journey? (He worked.)
- In missionary work today, when is it possible to be self-supporting and when is it not possible? (Missionaries from the US are not allowed to be self-supporting because in most West African countries

they have to sign documents saying they will not work.)

CPM Concepts[206]: How many of these apply or do not apply to the stories we have heard?

- *From 10 Universal Elements: 1, 2, 4, 5. 6. 7.8. 9. 10. (See list in 1st Story)*

- *From 10 Common Factors: 1. 2. 3. 4. 5. 5. 7. 8. 8. 10. (See list in 1st Story)*

- *From POUCH: 1. 2. 3. 4. (See list in 1st Story)*

- *From MAWL: 1. 2. 3. 4. (See list in 1st Story)*

What is God saying to us through His Word?

Conclusion

At the beginning we stated that our book would focus primarily on three target groups: 1) People who have not been involved in Bible Storying and want to utilize it as a church planting strategy from the beginning of the process; 2) People who are using Bible Storying as an initial strategy and want to proceed seamlessly from a storying group to a vibrant church; and 3) People who want to explore the possibility of utilizing Bible Storying in combination with other church planting methodologies.

In an effort to accomplish, this we developed four chapters: 1) Equipping the Storyer; 2) Understanding the Cultural Setting; 3) Developing the Strategies; and 4) Selecting the Stories. If Bible storyers are going to be effective church planters it is absolutely for them to have a solid biblical foundation, a harvest theology, a vision for church planting, a purposeful plan, a knowledge of church planting models, an awareness to avoid literate overhang, a willingness to retell the stories repeatedly, a desire to stick to the fundamentals, and an unwavering commitment to start churches.

To have an adequate understanding of the cultural context of the ministry focus group, Bible storyers need to conduct a worldview analysis, to study the communal worship patterns, to assess the levels and functions of orality, and to ascertain the perceptions that the people group has regarding literacy and Bible storying. Attempting to do Bible storying without having an understanding of the cultural context of the people group will generally lead to lack of effectiveness in church planting efforts. Trying to transplant material that has been developed in other settings without adapting to the local group will not get the job done.

Developing contextualized strategies requires adaptability regarding the manner in which the Bible stories are presented, regarding the number of stories that are told, regarding the story sets that are developed, regarding the places in which people meet, and regarding the methodology that is employed. In order to be effective church planters, Bible storyers need a biblical definition of church planting, the ability to fast track when it is necessary, a sensitivity to know when to draw the net, an ability to create a sense of community among the believers, a plan to incorporate the new converts into a group of worshippers, the skill to lead the people from a Bible storying group to a congregation, and the ability to train leaders. In order to ensure continuity of the congregation that has been started the Bible storyer needs to plan an exit strategy that involves shadow storying, expecting accountability from the leaders, enabling the leaders to carry on the work and dependence upon the Holy Spirit to guide in every step of the church planting process.

The goal of Chapter 4 has been to provide Bible storyers with resources that will help them to be more effective in leading those in their people groups to start many churches for the honor and glory of God. In the first part of this chapter we emphasized the fact that the seeds for church planting need to be planted in the early stages of the Evangelism Track. This allows people to progress smoothly and seamlessly from the Evangelism Track to the Church Planting Track. In the second part we have shared two church planting story sets. It is our hope that materials from each of these sets (used individually or combined) will encourage Bible storyers to develop contextualized sets that focus specifically on church planting. Even though we have provided complete story sets we cannot emphasize enough the importance of studying the people group's worldview and adapting the content as well as the presentation of the stories so these will be understood and applied by the recipients.

In the last portion of our book we have provided appendices specifically designed to help Bible storyers to get a better grasp of the church planting task and to design personalized strategies to become even more effective in their ministry.

At the outset we stated that the first purpose of this book was to explore ways in which Bible Storying can be more effective in planting churches among people groups and population segments throughout the world.[207] It is our sincere hope that this discussion has stimulated and inspired our readers to be instrumental in starting many more churches among the people groups and population segments where they serve.

It is also our desire that this book encourages on-going dialog leading to the development of even more effective church planting strategies through Bible Storying. We are keenly aware of the fact that more churches are being started than we are aware of, that there are effective strategies that we have not learned about yet, and that there are insights, observations, and suggestions that we need to consider. In light of this, on-going research, experimentation, and sharing are essential in order for all of us involved in Bible Storying to continue to learn and to be more effective in starting contextualized churches in our respective fields. We, therefore, encourage you to stay in touch with us and with other Bible storyers as we work together to fulfill the Great Commission among oral learners throughout the world. To God be the glory!

Appendix A:
Assessment of Storyer's Equipment

Item	Assessment Scale				
Biblical Foundation	1	2	3	4	5
Orality in Scripture	1	2	3	4	5
Great Commission & CP	1	2	3	4	5
CP Patterns	1	2	3	4	5
Harvest Theology	1	2	3	4	5
Vision for Church Planting	1	2	3	4	5
Purposeful Plan	1	2	3	4	5
Knowledge of C P Models	1	2	3	4	5
Willingness to Retell Stories	1	2	3	4	5
Sticking to the Fundamentals	1	2	3	4	5
Unwavering Commitment	1	2	3	4	5

List areas where improvement is needed:

_____

_____

_____

_____

_____

_____

_____

_____

_____

_____

_____

Indicate type of activity that can allow storyers to obtain information/experience:

Course: _____

Workshop: _____

Mentorship: _____

Self-Study: _____

Other: _____

Appendix B:
Orality/Storying Assessment

Storying History

1 ------------- 2 ------------- 3 -------------- 4 -------------- 5

Indicate the extent of storying present in this people group. Do they customarily tell stories (heritage stories, life stories, other)?

Mental Retention Capacity

1 ------------- 2 ------------- 3 -------------- 4 -------------- 5

Indicate the mental retention capacity of individuals in this people group. Are they able to re-tell the story after hearing two or three times? If not, what should you do to help them retain? More repetition?, Audio cassettes?, Mega Voice? Other _____?

(See Appendix L for resources that can aid mental retention)

Group Participation

1 ------------- 2 ------------- 3 -------------- 4 -------------- 5

Indicate the level at which individuals speak (talk, share) in the context of a group

Gender Participation

1 ------------- 2 ------------- 3 -------------- 4 -------------- 5

Indicate the level at which individuals participate in discussions in groups that have members of the opposite gender. What options do you have: a) Help them to get used to it? b) Meet in separate groups? Separate groups initially but get them together later?

Appendix C:
Assessment of Cultural Understanding

On this scale of 1 to 5 (this being the highest indicator) evaluate the following factors:

Factor   **Analysis**

Worldview analysis (how well do I know it?)

1 ------------- 2 ------------- 3--------------4--------------5

Briefly describe their worldview:

_____

_____

_____

_____

_____

_____

_____

_____

_____

Some bridges:

_____

_____

_____

_____

_____

_____

_____

_____

_____

_____

Some barriers:

_____

_____

_____

_____

_____

_____

_____

Communal worship patterns _(how well do I know them?)_

1 ------------- 2 ------------- 3-------------- 4--------------5

Briefly describe their worship patterns:

_____

_____

_____

_____

_____

_____

Briefly describe your strategy to reach each of these segments of your people group:

_____

_____

_____

_____

_____

_____

Appendix D[208]

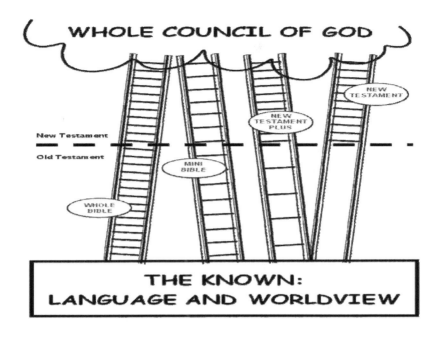

1) There is only one God; 2) God is holy and righteous; 3) God is creator and ruler; 4) God knows everything; 5) God can do anything; 6) God gives us everything we need; 7) God speaks through his word; 8) God keeps his promises; 9) God loves us and wants to be our friend; 10) God hates sin and separates himself from it; 11) God punishes all sin with death; 12) We choose to sin against God; 13) We answer to God for all that we do; 14) We cannot do anything to escape God's punishment; 15) Only God's perfect sacrifice can remove sin; 16) Jesus is God's perfect sacrifice; 17) We are saved by believing that Jesus died in our place.[209]

This is a brief list of the numerous core beliefs listed in the "Whole Council of God" found in the Bible.

The Kingdom of Heaven

12. Salvation by faith ???

11. Jesus, the Atonement ???

10. Only God's perfect sacrifice / can atone for man's sin.

OLD TESTAMENT

9.

8. Man is a sinner, separated from God by his sin.

7. Man is accountable to God for all he says and does.

6. God punishes sin by eternal separation from Him

5. God is holy, righteous, and hates sin.

4. God loves man and wants fellowship with Him.

3. God communicates with man and keeps His Word.

2. God is our all powerful, all knowing Provider.

1. God is one God, Sovereign, Creator, acting in history.

Jewish Worldview

Appendix F[211]

THE KINGDOM OF HEAVEN

17. GO TO PURGATORY ?

16. WORKS SALVATION?

1. NO ASSURANCE OF SALVATION

14 **NONBIBLICAL DOCTRINES**

13 SALVATION THROUGH THE CHURCH

12 SALVATION THROUGH SACRAMENTS

11 MARY – CO-MEDIATRIX.

10 IMMACULATE CONCEPTION OF MARY

9

8 **BIBLICAL DOCTRINES**

7 JESUS ASCENDED TO HEAVEN

6 JESUS AROSE FROM THE DEAD

5 JESUS DIED ON THE CROSS

4 JESUS BORN OF THE VIRGIN MARY

3 THE BIBLE IS GOD'S WORD

2 THE HOLY TRINITY

1 GOD IS THE CREATOR

ROMAN CATHOLIC WORLDVIEW

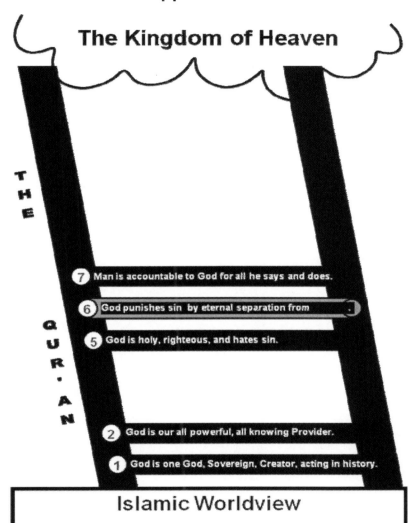

The Kingdom of Heaven

THE QUR·AN

7 Man is accountable to God for all he says and does.

6 God punishes sin by eternal separation from

5 God is holy, righteous, and hates sin.

2 God is our all powerful, all knowing Provider.

1 God is one God, Sovereign, Creator, acting in history.

Islamic Worldview

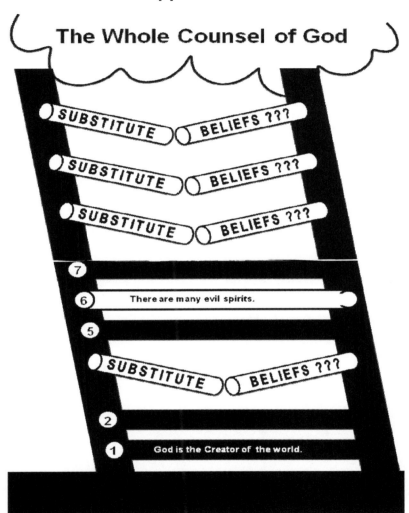

ANIMISTIC WORLDVIEW

Appendix I:
Strategy Development Analysis

On this scale of 1 to 5 (this being the highest indicator) indicate where you are with regard to each of the factors listed below.

Factor	Analysis				
Adaptability in presentation	1	2	3	4	5
Adaptability in number of stories	1	2	3	4	5
Adaptability in story sets	1	2	3	4	5
Adaptability in meeting place	1	2	3	4	5
Adaptability in methodology	1	2	3	4	5
Biblical definition of church	1	2	3	4	5
Fast tracking	1	2	3	4	5
Drawing the net	1	2	3	4	5
Sense of community	1	2	3	4	5
Incorporation	1	2	3	4	5
Transitioning to church	1	2	3	4	5
Training leaders	1	2	3	4	5
Adequate timing	1	2	3	4	5
Shadow storying	1	2	3	4	5
Avoiding dependency	1	2	3	4	5
Establishing accountability	1	2	3	4	5
Timely Exit	1	2	3	4	5
Depending on the Holy Spirit	1	2	3	4	5

Appendix J:
Specific Church Planting Steps

Utilizing this outline (discussed more fully in Chapter 1) design a specific plan for church planting through the use of Bible Storying. Indicate action plans to accomplish each of the objectives listed here:

Audience Contacted (Indicate your plans to contact groups for CBS)

Gospel Communicated (List Bible Stories you plan to use in Evangelism Track)

Hearers Converted (Indicate your plans to lead people to conversion)

Believers Congregated (Indicate your plans to gather people into worship groups)

Faith Confirmed (Indicate stories you plan to use in Discipleship Track)

Leaders Consecrated (Indicate your plan to find and train church leaders)

Believers Commended (Indicate plans for an exit strategy)

Appendix K:
Discovering Worldview Issues and Processing Worldview Information
Discovering Worldview Issues

- Observable Issues—Everyday practice and response of a people to their circumstances or what they do when something happens or goes wrong. (Who is in control?)

- Attend or observe their rituals—especially the rites of passage and their worship. (Most find comfort and assurance in ritual. Note the ritual leaders)

- Consider or verify generally held knowledge and attitudes toward the Bible, Christianity, God, Jesus, sin, forgiveness of those who wrong you. (Do they practice forgiveness, restitution, retaliation or revenge?)

- Look for perceived need where a people see themselves as needy and possibly open to new information to relieve that need. (ESL, literacy, sanitation, child care, agriculture)

- Look at newspapers and periodicals—issues are often brought up and discussed in media. Print media generally deal with longer standing issues, broadcast media more recent or urgent.)

- Look for NGO studies related to implementing changes in agriculture, nutrition, health, birth and child care, literacy, and education, cooperatives, and other efforts to improve a people's life.

- Look for dissertations and formal anthropological studies already done on a people.

- Conduct informal interviews with new believers and with segmented groups representing the population—men and women, old people, farmers, students, religious leaders, other opinion leaders, etc. (Pastors are often not good sources of this information.)

- Study apologetical publications (tracts, books and booklets about witness to a people's religion. (Be aware of the difference between classical religion and folk religion.)
- Network with other Christian agencies at work among the people to exchange worldview information.
- Visit internet websites by governments, educational, development, prayer and church groups.

Processing Worldview Information

- Look for correlation between issues—what do people do when there is sickness, demon possession, drought or famine?
- Look for trends—Some worldview issues are non-negotiable and therefore not subject to much change over time: taboos, deeply rooted cultural practices and those dealing with social relationships.
- Other worldview issues are undergoing change or are likely to change—unstable or no longer seen to be satisfactory explanations for life events: Westernization, secularizing trends, old ways are no longer relevant, "our gods have failed us."
- Look for positive and negative attitudes stemming from their worldview and restate as Barriers or Bridges to the Gospel, or if unbiased as Gaps in their knowledge.
- Assume a priority—those issues which immediately affect a hearing and acceptance of Gospel information.
- Reserve less important issues (or those requiring more teaching and acceptance of basics) for discipling and maturing.
- Be prepared to alter the priority of issues and to add any new issues discovered during the storying strategy.
- Also set aside any issues which do not prove to be troublesome or relevant.

- Use this worldview information to inform and instruct the presentation of the Gospel as the issues relate to the biblical truths leading to salvation, planting a church, discipling, maturing and training leadership.

Dealing With Worldview Issues In Bible Storying

1. *CHALLENGE*: **Apologetically Dispute or Debate, Presenting the Facts and Targeting Beliefs Which are Biblically in Error. (Win/Lose)**

2. *AVOID TEMPORARILY*: **Avoid Dealing with Issues Until a More Satisfactory Time When More Truth is in Place Through Additional Stories.**

3. *BUILD A BETTER TRUTH*: **No Debate; Displace Existing Beliefs With Better Beliefs Through Stories—Those That are More Consistent (according to their logic) or Which Better Answer the Unanswered Questions in their Worldview. (Win/Win)**

Final Words

- **Do not get hung up learning everything about a people—you can't.**

- **Many worldviews today are dynamic and changing, accelerating in change.**

- **Do not put off beginning your Bible Storying relationship with a people—you will learn from them as you go.**

- **Knowing the essential worldview information will help you to avoid serious communication problems leading to broken relationships and help you to find the "open doors" of receptivity and understanding leading to faith in Christ and CPM.**

- **Knowing a people's key worldview issues helps you to pray specifically for them. Do not give up when it seems that key issues elude you—with one SE Asia people it took several years to** finally kind a key issue that unlocked a door—a fear of death!

- Many worldview issues are revealed in pre-story dialog and post-story dialog and comment/reaction to the Bible stories by listeners. Pay close attention to these comments and questions.

- Keep good notes and consider using what you have learned to train those who come to work with you or to follow you.

- Look for opportunities to share what you have learned with your network of Great Commission colleagues.

Appendix L:
Resources for Bible Storying

Bible Story Quilts

Carla Joy Clements of *Visual Story Bible Ministries* of Moultrie, GA, is promoting Bible Story quilts that tell in picture format the stories from *God & Man*. On her website she offers the patterns and the stories to accompany each pane of the quilt. Check out her website at www.BibleQuilt.org.

Bible Story Pictures

Good News

A set of 40 pictures available in large (flipchart). Medium and small (pocket size) formats, accompanied by recorded commentary (available in more than 900 languages. www.globalrecordings.net

The Living Christ

A set of 120 loose leaf, A4 size pictures based on the life of Christ with accompanying recorded commentary. www.gospelrecordings.net

Telling the Story

A set of 105 pictures used in chronological approaches to teaching. www.csm-publishing.net or New Tribes Mission www.ntmbooks.com/index.jsp?categoryid=61

Solar-Powered Technology

MegaVoice Ambassador

The MegaVoice Ambassador is a palm-sized, self-contained digital audio player with a rechargeable solar panel and can be used individually with an ear phone or in a group setting using a built-in speaker. It contains custom content which cannot be erased by the end user. It is built in such a way that it can be used in remote, harsh conditions. For more information write: www.megavoice.com

The following are among the ministries using this powerful technological tool:

God's Story Project

Audio resources

The God's Story Project, led by Dorothy A. Miller utilizes the MegaVoice Ambassador and has chronological storytelling presentations (Old Testament and New Testament) in over 200 languages. Information can be obtained through e-mail: info@gods-story.org or through their website www.Gods-Story.org

Video resources

God´s Story: From Creation to Eternity, is a series of 14 Bible stories presented in a video format. It is available in several languages and comes with a script that is designed to assist the storyers. It can be obtained through: www.Gods-Story.org

Evangelist Backpack

The Evangelist Backpack contains a portable DVD player, a compact battery power source, a light, a folding solar panel, a VCD of God's Story, and a padded backpack. Information can be obtained through:

info@gods-story.org

Solar Fix-Tuned Radios

These radios that operate on solar energy are programmed to tune in on a specific frequency guaranteeing that the listeners will hear only the programs broadcast by Christian radio stations.

GALCOM

GALCOM has sent over 570,000 fix-tuned radios to 125 countries including Northern Iraq, Burkina Faso, Tanzania, and the Sudan. For information, contact GALCOM galcom@galcom.org

Radio Bible Project

The Radio Bible Project is a global partnership between Hosanna/Faith Commeth By Hearing, the International Bible

Society, TransWorld Radio, and the United Bible Societies formed to bring the Word of God to oral societies. The Radio Bible consists of 365 fifteen minute broadcasts of stories from the Bible. For more information contact: www.globalrecordings.net

Web-Based Resources

www.augusthouse.com – Children's books, folktale anthologies, and stories for classroom use.

www.biblestorytelling.org – A Bible Storytelling project that uses Bible Stories for the purpose of evangelizing, teaching, preaching, planting churches, and training church leaders.

www.christianstorytelling.com – Networks with Christian storytellers to nurture storytelling in the Christian community

www.chronologicalbiblestorying.com – The official Chronological Bible Storying website which contains helpful resources.

www.OneStory.org – A joint venture of four mission sending agencies: Campus Crusade, International Mission Board, Wycliff International, and Youth With A Mission. It provides information on Quest, Venture, and Journey options.

www.nobs,org – Network of Bible Storytellers, develops resources for telling biblical stories.

www.internationaloralitynetwork.com – A network of mission agencies that conducts consultations and training workshops for learners and experienced storytellers.

www.OralStrategies.com – A website primarily supporting oral strategies and orality needs related to evangelism and church planting. Especially helpful are the articles, resources and links to other sites and resources.

biblestorying@sbcglobal.net – A resource address operated by J.O.Terry (one of the pioneers in Chronological Bible Storying) that provides an Electronic Newsletter, a Journal of Bible Storying, and information on workshops to train workers for CBS ministries.

www.progressivevision.org Dr. Avery T. Willis Jr. has directed the "Following Jesus" project which consists of a number of CDs prepared by Advanced Media for Discipling Oral Communicators.

www.t4global.org The founders of T4 Global, Chuck Madinger and Pete McLain have developed oral strategies to communicate information related to health, civic education, human rights, and agriculture as well as evangelism, discipleship, pastor training. As a faith-based spin off from Voice for Humanity, this ministry had touched the lives of millions in numerous countries.

www.fjseries.org – A seven module series of recorded discussions and Bible stories for evangelism and discipleship.

Recommended Books

Garrison, David, Church Planting Movements: How God Is Redeeming A Lost World.: Wit Take Resources, 2004.

Kreider, Larry, House Church Networks. House to House Publications, 2001.

Lovejoy, Grant, ed., Making Disciples of Oral Learners. International Orality Network, 2005

Steffen, Tom A., Passing the Baton: Church Planting That Empowers. La Habra: Center for Organizational & Ministry Development, 1993

Sanchez, Daniel R., et. al., Starting Reproducing Congregations. Church Starting Network, 2001, www.churchstarting.net

Sanchez, Daniel R., ed., Church Planting Movements in North America. Church Starting Network. 2006, www.churchstarting.net

Seymour, Bruce D., Creating Stories That Connect. Kregel, 2007.

Terry, J.O., Basic Bible Storying, Church Starting Network, 2006, www.churchstarting.net

Rod Zdero, The Global House Church Movement. William Carey Library, 2004.

Endnotes

---

[1] Dr. Jim Slack was instrumental in developing the *Chronological Bible Storying* model that was so named to distinguish it from *Chronological Bible Teaching*, *Chronological Bible Storytelling*, and *God and Man Storytelling*. For a brief history of the emergence and development of Chronological Bible Storying see, Dr. Jim Slack, "How the International Mission Board Got Involved in Orality Strategies and Especially Chronological Bible Storying," unpublished paper, December, 2007 JSlack@imb.org. For further clarification on the distinction between Chronological Bible Teaching, Chronological Bible Storytelling, and Chronological Bible Storying see, James Byron Slack, *The Development of a Chronological Bible Storying Workshop Module For Use in Training Literates to Communicate the Gospel Among Oral Communicators*, Doctor of Ministry Dissertation, Southwestern Baptist Theological Seminary, 1995, 32-35, see also J.O. Terry, *Basic Bible Storying*, Church Starting Network, 2006, 140-45.

[2] The term Chronological Bible Storying (CBS) has become a trademark for the model of Bible Storying that was developed by Jim Slack, J.O. Terry, and others connected with the International Mission Board. When the emerging methodology was being worked out, the term "Storying" was substituted in place of "Teaching" to make a statement that the Bible stories were the primary mode of chronologically presenting God's Word. Teaching would still take place, but it would follow the Storying mode, and where teaching was prohibited or limited by circumstances and gatekeepers, the stories could still be told. Since Chronological Bible Storying is most often the strategic form of Bible Storying used in initiating Church Planting Movements, that term or its shorter form CBS will be used repeatedly in this book. In other instances in which different storying models are being employed we will use the broader term "Bible Storying." To the extent that it is possible we will seek to differentiate between these two terms.

[3] David Barrett, *Our Globe And How To Reach It*, (Birmingham, Alabama: New Hope 1990), 25 ,28. See also, Grant Lovejoy, making disciples of oral learners, International Orality Network, 2005, 3.

[4] Jim Slack points out that *Chronological Bible Storying* was developed as a model for use in evangelism, discipleship, church planting, and pastoral mentoring of oral communicators and learners whether or not they ever learned to read and write and become literate communicators and learners. See, Dr. Jim Slack,

"How the International Mission Board Got Involved in Orality Strategies and Especially Chronological Bible Storying," unpublished paper, December, 2007 JSlack@imb.org.

[5] LaNette, Thompson, written correspondence with Dr. Grant Lovejoy, May 9, 2006.

[6] Wayne Dye, "The Literacy Hypothesis and Storying: Toward a better theory." December 2, 2007, 1.

[7] This is an example of Bible storying that is not chronological but situational. Even though the term "chronological" is used (e.g., Chronological Bible Storying), we are committed to utilizing storying in a variety of ways. Depending on the setting, we can use "thematic," "situational," and "slice of life" storying to share the gospel. It is not unusual for one approach to open the door for more extended, chronological storying.

[8] This experience was shared with Daniel R. Sanchez by one of his former students who will remain anonymous for security reasons.

[9] J.O. Terry, speaking about the experiences of his team working in Asia.

[10] Mark Snowden, director, Mission Education Team, North American Mission Board, SBC, Written correspondence, July, 2007.

[11] Keith Stamps, written correspondence with Daniel R. Sanchez, August 22, 2007.

[12] Donald Barger, written correspondence with Daniel R. Sanchez, November 8, 2007

[13] Steven King, written correspondence with Daniel R. Sanchez, August 23, 2007.

[14] Jeremy Taliaferro, e-mail sent to Daniel R. Sanchez, October 25, 2007.

[15] Electronic letter sent to Daniel R. Sanchez by Fernando and Brenda Larzabal serving in South America, October 1, 2007.

[16] Christian J. Ammons, e-mail sent to J.O. Terry, October 25, 2007.

17 Johnny Norwood Report, cited in J.O. Terry, **Bible Storying** God's Word Story by Story to Empower Every Person Oral or Literate for Witness and Discipling Their Own, October, 2007, Vol. 14 No 4

[18] Rick Brown, "Brother Jacob and Master Isaac: How One Insider Movement Began," *International Journal of Frontier Missiology*, 24:1, Spring, 2007, 41.

[19] Ibid.

[20] Ibid.

[21] It is inspiring to learn about the way in which Bible Storying is resulting in the establishment of many churches in many parts of the world. The concern is for those areas where sincere Bible Storying efforts are being made yet, these are not leading to the starting of new congregations.

[22] This segment has been taken from, Daniel R. Sanchez, Ebbie Smith, *Starting Reproducing Congregations* (Church Starting Network, 2000). Used by permission.

[23] Gordon D. Fee and Douglas Stuart, *How To Read The Bible For All Its Worth*, Grand Rapids: Zondervan, 1982, 73.

[24] Richard Bauckham, *Jesus and the Eyewitnesses: The Gospel as Eyewitness Testimony*, (Grand Rapids: William B. Eerdmans Publishing Co., 2006), 211.

[25] Ibid., 216, 17.

[26] Ibid., 217.

[27] See Bauckham's discussion of Papias' view, ibid., 221.

[28] Ibid., 230

[29] J. Dewey, "Oral Methods of Structuring Narratives in Mark," *Int* 53 (1989) 32-44, cited in Bauckham, op. cit., 232-233.

[30] Joanna Dewey, "The Survival of Mark's Gospel: A Good Story?" *JBL*, 123 (2004), 499, cited in Bauckham, op. cit., 233.

[31] Bauckham, op. cit, 230.

32. Alexander Rattray Hay, The New Testament Order for Church and Missionary (Audubon, NJ: New Testament Missionary Union, 1947), 53.

33. David Hesselgrave, *Planting Churches Cross-Culturally* (Grand Rapids, MI: Baker Book House, 1980).

[34] David Hesselgrave's outline has been used in this discussion which appears in Daniel R. Sanchez, Ebbie Smith, Curt Watke, *Starting Reproducing Congregations*, Church Starting Network, 2000. Used by permission.

[35] Ebbie C. Smith, Growing Healthy Churches: New Directions for Church Growth in the 21st Century, Church Starting Network, 2003, 24.

[36] To obtain valuable information on this see, Tom A. Steffen, *Passing the Baton: Church Planting That Empowers*, (La Habra: Center for Organizational & Ministry Development, 1993),

[37] Donald, McGavran, *Understanding Church Growth* (Grand Rapids: William Eerdmans Publishing Co., 1970), 34.

[38]Ibid., 40-44.

[39] This is not an argument against ministry to meet human needs. It is an argument against believing that the task has been completed when the human needs are met without regard for the spiritual condition of people.

[40] Ebbie C. Smith, *Growing Healthy Churches*, Church Starting Network, 2003, 74.

[41] Keith Stamps, written correspondence to Daniel R. Sanchez, April 18, 2008.

[42] The material that follows has been taken and adapted with permission from the book *Starting Reproducing Congregations*, Church Starting Network, 2001.

43. See, George Barna, *The Power of Vision* (Ventura: Regal Books, 1992).

44. Barna, *The Power of Vision*, 28.

45. Ibid., 27.

46.Dale E. Galloway, 20/ 20 Vision: *How to Create A Successful Church With Lay Pastors And Cell Groups*, Portland: Scott Publishing Company, 1986, 30.

47. Aubry Malphurs, *Planting Growing Churches for the 21st Century* (Grand Rapids: Baker, 1992), 239.

48. Ibid., p. 239. For a more extensive discussion of this see Aubrey Malphurs, *Vision for Ministry in the 21st Century* (Grand Rapids: Baker, 1992), 31-39.

[49] Daniel R. Sanchez, et. al., *Starting Reproducing Congregations*, Fort Worth: Church Starting Network, 2001, www.churchstarting.net. With the authors' permission portions of chapter 5 of this book will be utilized in this segment.

[50] Ibid.

51. George Paterson and Richard Scoggins, *Church Multiplication Guide* (Pasadena: William Carey Library, 1993), 12.

52. Ibid., p. 15.

53. Claylan Coursey, *How Churches Can Start Churches* (Nairobi: Baptist Publishing House, 1084).

54. Ibid., 14.

55. Paterson, 7.

56. Ibid., 7.

57 David Garrison, *Church Planting Movements: How God is Redeeming A Lost World* (Richmond, Virginia: WIG Take Resources, 2004), 22.

58. James B. Slack, "Initiating Church Planting Movements among Peoples on the Frontiers of Lostness," paper presented at the joint meeting of EMS and ISFM, November, 1997.

59. Ibid, 1.

60. Timothy C. Tennent, "Training Missionaries to Resistant Peoples," paper presented at the joint meeting of EMS and ISFM, November 22, 1997, p. 3.

61 For a more extensive description see Garrison, *Church Planting Movements: How God Is Redeeming A Lost World*.

62. Raymond Fung, *Households of God on China's Soil* (New York: Orbis Books, 1982), x.

63 For additional information on Cell-Based churches, review Harold Bullock's chapter, "From Cell-Based Churches to Church Planting Movements" in Daniel R. Sanchez, ed., *Church Planting Movements in North America,* (Ft. Worth, Texas: Church Starting Network, 2007.

64 Rod Zdero, *The Global House Church Movement,* Pasadena: William Carey Library, 2004), 21.

65 Ibid., 21.

66 Some prefer to use the term "simple church." We use the term "basic church" to convey the idea that these types of churches, even though small, can carry out the basic functions of a church described in Acts 2:40-47.

67 David Garrison, *Church Planting Movements*, 22.

68 Harold Bullock, op. cit.

69 David Garrison, *Church Planting Movements*, 35.

70 T4T Training For Trainers: Oral-Preference Learners Version is an unpublished document produced by the Saddleback Valley Community Church, Lake Forrest, California.

71 Grant Lovejoy, written correspondence with LaNette Thompson, May 9, 2006.

72 T4T Training For Trainers: Oral-Preference Learners Version is an unpublished document produced by the Saddleback Valley Community Church, Lake Forrest, California.

73 Jim Slack is concerned that if storyers are not cautious they will end up utilizing literate methods that have the potential of undermining oral strategies. Slack, interviewed by Daniel Sanchez, October 2, 2007

74 Grant Lovejoy, written correspondence with LaNette Thompson, May 9, 2006.

75 J.O. Terry, Bible Storying Newsletter, July 1999, Vol. 6, No. 3

76 Steven King, written correspondence with Daniel R. Sanchez, August 23, 2007.

77 Keith Stamps, written correspondence with Daniel R. Sanchez, August 22, 2007.

78 Ken Sorrell, written correspondence with Daniel R. Sanchez, August, 2007.

79 Ibid.

80 Paul F. Koehler, posted note on International Orality Network, March 29, 2008.

81 We are seeing more use of Bible storying as components of other strategies. Bible Storying is now strongly coupled with the Orality issue and with Scripture Access for mother tongue speakers. Discipling is an ongoing need in these oral learner churches. J.O. Terry, speaking about his experiences in the Philippines.

82 For more information see J.O. Terry, *Basic Bible Storying*, 136-39.

83 J.O. Terry, sharing experiences from the mission field.

84 Grant Lovejoy, written correspondence with LaNette Thompson, May 9, 2006.

[85] Keith Stamps, written correspondence with Daniel R. Sanchez, August 22, 2007.

[86] Charles Madinger, Derek C. Eggers and Kyle McClellan, "Why Orality Works: Insights from field experience," A paper prepared for the International Orality Network ION Conference, 2007, ii.

[87] Jeremy Taliaferro, e-mail sent to Daniel R. Sanchez, October 25, 2007.

[88] James Brandt, *Bringing the Written Word to the World*, MLP Newsletter 44, June 2007

[89] *OneStory Report, Global PrayerGram July 07*

[90] Ed Beach, comment posted on International Orality Network, December 8, 1007.

[91] Ed Beach, comment posted on International Orality Network, December 10, 1007.

[92] This summary of ten basic steps for CBS was prepared by Mark Snowden. Unpublished Power Point presentation.

[93] See J.O. Terry, *Basic Bible Storying*, 2006; Grant Lovejoy, *Making Disciples of Oral Learners*, International Orality Network, 2005; James B. Slack, J.O. Terry, Grant Lovejoy, *Chronological Bible Storying: A Methodology for Presenting the Gospel to Oral Communicators* (Richmond, Virginia: International Mission Board, 2004). See also "Recommended Books" in appendix L.

[94] See, Louis J. Luzbetak, *The Church And Cultures* (Pasadena: William Carey Library, 1970), 351.

[95] LaNette, Thompson, e-mail to Daniel R. Sanchez, September 6, 2007

[96] The term "illiterate" carries with it a condescending tone which is resented by oral learners in many parts of the world. It also fails to take into account, as Weber himself points out, that oral communicators can be quite capable of learning if the proper communication methods are employed.

[97] H.R. Weber, *The Communication of the Gospel to Illiterates* (London: SCN PRESS LTD, 1957), 18.

[98] Ibid., 19, 28, 30.

[99] Ibid., 70, 71.

[100] Jeremy Taliaferro, e-mail sent to Daniel R. Sanchez, October 25, 2007.

[101] Keith Stamps, written correspondence with Daniel R. Sanchez, August 22, 2007.

[102] In his article, "Corporate Storytelling: Tell and Learn," Michael T. Adams defines "andragogy" as a model of adult instruction (almost the opposite of pedagogy) in which the student plays a large part of what is being taught largely through the use of stories. For more information see: Michael T. Abrams Website: www.storyteller.net/tellers/mabrams

[103] J.O. Terry, sharing his observations from his field experience.

[104] Jim Slack, Lewis Myers, "Constructing A worldview," To The Edge, April 2005 USA & UPG Site Edition, Appendix C, 169.

[105] Jim Slack, Global Evangelism and Church Growth Consultant, IMB, SBC, May 2004 Edition/Revised June 8, 2004 Edition.

[106] It must be kept in mind however, that many people who claim they are Catholics also are involved in many Animistic practices and therefore employ a syncretistic approach. Still others identify themselves as Catholics yet have basically a materialistic lifestyle.

[107] Jim Slack, personal conversation with Dr. Grant Lovejoy, recorded by Dr. Lovejoy, May 9, 2006.

[108] Christy Brawner, Good News of Jesus: Storying the Gospel of Matthew. brawner@pobox.com

[109] Christy Brawner, Beginning a New Life in Christ: Storying the Gospel of Matthew. brawner@pobox.com

[110] J.O.Terry, conversation reconstructed from actual account with a Kui listener, 1994.

[111] Tom Dyson, www.geocities.com/thedysonfamily/

[112] J.O.Terry, "Worldview Inventory Questionnaire." For a more extensive study of this subject see J.O. Terry, Basic Bible Storying, 39-48.

[113] For excellent guidelines on worldview studies see, Jim Slack, Lewis Myers, To The Edge, USA & EPG Edition, (Richmond: International Mission Board, 2005 (or latest edition).

[114] Thora Broyles, e-mail sent to LaNette Thompson, May 12, 2006

[115] For a discussion of levels of orality see Jim Slack, Lewis Myers, To The Edge, USA & EPG Edition, (Richmond: International Mission Board, 2005 (or latest edition).

[116] LaNette, Thompson, e-mail to Daniel R. Sanchez, September 6, 2007

[117] G. Campbell Morgan, *The Great Physician,* Westwood, New Jersey: Fleming H. Revell Company, 1937, 7.

[118] Ibid., In his book Morgan recounts the stories of 50 persons who directly or indirectly had an encounter with the Great Physician.

[119] Tom Stephen, *Passing the Baton*, 149.

[120] R.C.H. Lenski, Interpretation of I and II Corinthians, Minneapolis: Augsburg Publishing House, 1973, 376, 77.

[121] Ibid.

[122] ibid.. 149.

[123] Christy A. Brawner, *The Good News of Jesus: Storying the Gospel of Matthew,* Pioneer Evangelism Series. brawnew@pobox.com

[124] J.O. Terry speaking about his experiences on the mission field.

[125] J.O. Terry describing his experiences in East Asia.

[126] J.O. Terry speaking about his experiences on the mission field.

[127] Jeremy Taliaferro, op. cit.

[128] Donald Barger, op. cit.

[129] Thora Broyles, e-mail sent to LaNette Thompson, May 12, 2006

[130] J.O. Terry speaking about an experience he had on the field.

[131] Steve Flook, e-mail sent to Daniel R. Sanchez, November 17, 2007.

[132] J.O. Terry describing his experiences on the mission field.

[133] Our point here is not that these standards are inherently undesirable. Quite the contrary, it is a blessing to have good church buildings and formally trained leaders. What we are seeking to communicate is that in communities where the resources and conditions do not lend themselves to provide these, vibrant churches can still be established. Insisting on standards that are not necessarily biblical requirements can slow down if not kill church planting efforts in some areas. For more information see, David Garrison, Church Planting Movements, 49, 51.

[134] Article 6 of the 1963 and 2000 SBC "Baptist Faith and Message," cited in Daniel R. Sanchez, ed., *Church Planting Movements in North America*, Chapter 25, 7.

[135] Stan Norman, "Ecclesiological Guidelines to Inform Southern Baptist Church Planters," un-published paper, New Orleans Baptist Theological Seminary, September, 28, 4004.

[136] Larry Kreider, *House Church Networks: A church for a new generation* (Ephrata, PA: House to House Publications, 2001), 2.

[137] LaNette, Thompson, written correspondence with Dr. Grant Lovejoy, May 9, 2006.

[138] J.O. Terry describing his experiences on the mission field.

[139] J.O. Terry speaking about his experiences on the mission field.

[140] LaNette, Thompson, written correspondence with Dr. Grant Lovejoy, May 9, 2006.

[141] Grant Lovejoy, written correspondence with LaNette Thompson, May 9, 2006.

[142] Steven King, written correspondence with Daniel R. Sanchez, August 23, 2007.

[143] Paul F. Koehler, *Stories From Storytellers*, Storyteller123@gmail.com

[144] J.O. Terry speaking about his experiences on the mission field.

[145] J.O. Terry, sharing his experience on the mission field.

[146] Jeremy Taliaferro, e-mail sent to Daniel R. Sanchez, October 25, 2007.

[147] J.O. Terry, sharing his experiences on the mission field. For a more extensive study of this subject see J.O. Terry, *Basic Bible Storying*, 116-126.

[148] Charles Madinger, Derek C. Eggers and Kyle McClellan, "Why Orality Works: Insights from field experience," A paper prepared for the International Orality Network ION Conference, 2007, ii.

[149] Grant Lovejoy, written correspondence with LaNette Thompson, May 9, 2006.

[150] H.R. Weber, op. cit., 49, 50.

[151] J.O. Terry speaking about his experiences in the Philippines and other Asian countries.

[152] J.O. Terry, sharing observations from his experience on the field.

[153] Grant Lovejoy, written correspondence with LaNette Thompson, May 9, 2006.

[154] Ibid.

[155] J.O. Terry speaking about his experiences in East Asia

[156] J.O. Terry speaking about his experiences on the mission field.

[157] Steven King, written correspondence with Daniel R. Sanchez, August 23, 2007.

[158] Keith Stamps, written correspondence with Daniel R. Sanchez, August 22, 2007.

[159] Tom A. Steffen, *Passing the Baton*, 133-134.

[160] Keith Stamps, written correspondence with Daniel R. Sanchez, August 22, 2007.

[161] Grant Lovejoy, written correspondence with LaNette Thompson, May 9, 2006.

[162] Here we are employing the terminology currently being used by literacy experts to designate the various stages of literacy at which adults find themselves. Robert M Hauser, Christopher F. Edley Jr., Judith Anderson Koenig, and Stuart W. Elliot, Executive Summary "Measuring Literacy: Performance Levels for Adults, Interim Report," 6. National Academy of Science, www.nap.edu

[163] Focusing on orality is inherent in CBS methodology. The point we are making here is that an understanding of orality is crucial to the storying process among oral people.

[164] Thora Broyles, e-mail sent to LaNette Thompson, May 12, 2006

[165] Wayne Dye, "The Literacy Hypothesis and Storying: Toward a better theory," December 2, 2007, 1.

[166] Ed Beach, posted comments on International Orality Network, December 3, 2007.

[167] Paul F. Khoehler, posted notes on International Orality Network, March 29, 2008.

[168] Paul F. Khoehler, posted notes on International Orality Network, March 31, 2008.

[169] Electronic letter sent to Daniel R. Sanchez by Fernando and Brenda Larzabal serving in South America, October 1, 2007.

[170] Donald Barger, written correspondence with Daniel R. Sanchez, November 8, 2007.

[171] Jeremy Taliaferro, e-mail sent to Daniel R. Sanchez, October 25, 2007.

[172] Donald Barger, written correspondence with Daniel R. Sanchez, November 8, 2007.

[173] Charles Madinger, Why Orality Works," op cit, 13.

[174] *Beth Seversen, Hillcrest Covenant Church*

[175] J.O. Terry, sharing experiences on the mission field.

[176] H.R Weber, op. cit., 40.

[177] For more information on this see D. Bruce Seymour, Creating Stories That Connect, Kregel, 2007.

[178] Steven King, written correspondence with Daniel R. Sanchez, August 23, 2007.

[179] Ibid.

[180] Jackson Day, Bible Storytelling Tools: A Guide for Storying the Bible, La Vergne, TN: Lightning Source, 2007, 13.

[181] Steve Flook, e-mail sent to Daniel R. Sanchez, November 17, 2007.

[182] Ibid.

[183] LaNette, Thompson, e-mail to Daniel R. Sanchez, September 6, 2007

[184] LaNette, Thompson, e-mail to Daniel R. Sanchez, September 6, 2007

[185] J.O. Terry speaking about his experiences on the mission field.

[186] Trevor McIlwain, *Building on Firm Foundations*, New Tribes Mission, vol. 1, pp. 60-62. See also, Tom A. Steffen, *Passing the Baton: Church Planting That Empowers*, 133-134.

[187] Tom A. Steffen, *Passing the Baton: Church Planting That Empowers*.

[188] Steve Flook, e-mail sent to Daniel R. Sanchez, November, 17, 2007.

[189] The "tracks" focus on the various emphases of Chronological Bible Storying (e.g., Evangelism, Discipleship, Church Starting, and Leadership Training). The "story sets" are the stories that are selected under the "track" categories to address particular needs of a people group. For example, the Hope Story Set has been developed by J.O. Terry for the purpose of communicating the gospel to people who have experienced disasters. For more

information see J.O. Terry, Basic Bible Storying pp. 24-32; 138; 178-181.

[190] Avery T. Willis Jr., *Following Jesus: Living in the Family of Jesus*, Disc 5, Tracks 22-30., Advanced Media for Discipling Oral Communicators, www. Progressive Vision.org

[191] Ibid.

[192] Ibid.

[193] Dr. Jim Slack, "Chronology of Acts As Church Planting Model," unpublished Power Point Presentation prepared for CBS workshops.

[194] The foundational work that Dr. Jim Slack did as he addressed the topic of church planting was very helpful in preparing the list of stories for this portion of the chapter.

[195] All of the material in a composite story is found in the Bible, however, it is not found in just one place (e.g., a chapter or a book). The Bible storyer who puts together a composite story selects the various passages that deal with a particular person or event and pieces them together so that the listener will get the complete picture. Care should be given that the composite story is in harmony with all of the teachings of Scripture and that it communicates God's message to the listeners.

[196] See Avery Willis, Following Jesus: Living in the Family of Jesus, http//fjseries.org or www.ProgressiveVision.org. This two-part module includes 49 Bible story sessions. Each has been selected for training New Believers and starting Church Planting Movements in traditional oral cultures.

[197] Ibid.

[198] These concepts come from the booklet *Church Planting Movements* by David Garrison. October 1999. Office of Overseas Operations, International Mission Board of the Southern Baptist Convention, P.O. Box 6767, Richmond, VA 23230-0767.

[199] Ibid., 33-36.

[200] Ibid., 37-40.

[201] Ibid., 43, 60.

[202] Ibid., 44, 60.

[203] Ibid., 49-52.

[204] We want to emphasize once again that the fact that we are including a long list of questions does not mean that the storyer

needs to use all of them. This list simply helps the storyer to be aware of the questions that are pertinent to a story. Knowledge of the people group's worldview, level of comprehension, retention capacity, etc. will help the storyer, after prayer and meditation to decide which questions to use in each case.

[205] These concepts come from the booklet *Church Planting Movements* by David Garrison.

[206] These concepts come from the booklet *Church Planting Movements* by David Garrison.

[207] It is inspiring to learn about the way in which Chronological Bible Storying is resulting in the establishment of many churches in many parts of the world. The concern is for those areas where sincere CBS efforts are being made yet, these are not leading to the starting of new congregations.

[208] This chart was designed by Lynne Abney Johnson, used by permission.

[209] For a more extensive study of this subject see J.O. Terry, *Basic Bible Storying*, Church Starting Network, 2006, 35-38.

[210] Ibid.

[211] This chart was adapted from the one designed by Lynne Abney Johnson. Used by permission

[212] This chart was designed by Lynne Abney Johnson, used by permission.

[213] Ibid.

Made in the USA
Lexington, KY
03 March 2011